MW01069430

DUCATI
DESMOQUATTRO
SUPERBIKES

IAN FALLOON

MBI Publishing Company

First published in 2002 by MBI Publishing
Company, Galtier Plaza, Suite 200,
380 Jackson Street, St. Paul, MN 55101-3885 USA

MBI Publishing Company books are also
available at discounts in bulk quantity for
industrial or sales-promotional use. For details
write to Special Sales Manager at Motorbooks
International Wholesalers & Distributors
Galtier Plaza, Suite 200, 380 Jackson Street,
St. Paul, MN 55101-3885 USA

Library of Congress Cataloging-in-Publication Data
ISBN 0-7603-1093-9

On the front cover: Ducati's 996R may have
looked like previous versions of the company's
mighty Superbike, but the all-new *Testastretta*
engine lurking beneath the carbon-fiber fairing
was the most potent powerplant ever produced by
the Italian firm. *Ian Falloon*

On the frontispiece: The final 888 Sport
Production was the delectable SP5. This offered
the performance of the 888 SPS in a slightly more
civilized package. *Rolf im Brahm*

On the title page: Almost as dominant as in 1995,
Fogarty easily won the 1999 World Superbike
Championship on the Ducati Performance 996.
Ian Falloon

On the back cover, Top: The first street version of
the *Desmoquattro* was the 1988 851 Strada. This
promised much but failed to deliver. The
Marvic/Akront 16-inch wheels contributed to
strange handling. *Ian Falloon*

Bottom: While the 996 looked outwardly similar
to the 1998 916, there was more to the new
model than simply a larger engine. *Australian
Motorcycle News*

Edited by Darwin Holmstrom
Designed by Tom Heffron
Layout by Bruce Leckie

Printed in China

Contents

Introduction and Acknowledgments

Undoubtedly, the Desmoquattro has been the most significant engine ever produced by Ducati, and also one of the greatest modern motorcycle engine designs. Prior to the Desmoquattro, Ducati had achieved the occasional stunning race result, but the company was really too small to make a huge global impact. This all changed in 1986 with the creation of the 748-cc, liquid-cooled four-valve desmodromic racer. For the first time, a twin-cylinder four-stroke was competitive against multicylinder racers. The design was also so far-reaching that continual development would see it reign for 15 years in Superbike racing.

The story of the Desmoquattro also epitomizes Ducati's approach to design and development. Throughout the history of the company, its philosophy has been evolution rather than revolution, and engines have always been designed for racing first and the street second. The bevel-drive twins of the early 1970s grew out of the overhead cam-shaft singles that had their roots in Ing. Fabio Taglioni's first Marianna of 1955. When Taglioni dreamed the Pantah in 1976, this too had strong links to the earlier twins and singles. Yet while the bevel-drive singles and twins were undoubted engineering marvels, their achievements pale into insignificance compared to the Desmoquattro. The Desmoquattro is unequivocally the most

successful Ducati ever. Essentially a Pantah with liquid-cooled four-valve cylinder heads, the latest 999 Testastretta retains strong links to earlier designs. This process of evolution has served Ducati well. While other companies experiment with different engine layouts, Ducati has managed to maintain its leadership, both on the race track and on the street, with a single basic design. Even the world at large knows of Ducati through the Desmoquattro's achievements, and few motorcycles can emulate it. Its incredible success is also a tribute to the brilliance of Ducati's engineers. But the Desmoquattro isn't just about racing. By the end of the year 2000, more than 60,000 Desmoquattro-powered production models were in circulation in various incarnations—from the 916 to the Monster S4 and ST4. Here is the story of all these motorcycles, one of the greatest designs of the present day, and possibly one of the finest of all time.

I would like to thank all who have assisted in researching this book and providing photographs. Ing. Massimo Bordi, the father of the Desmoquattro, has always politely answered my questions, and willingly given his time. He also provided his previously unpublished notes regarding the development of the 851 and 888 from 1986 through 1992. Gianluigi "Gigi" Mengoli, the current technical director at Ducati and responsible for the original Desmoquattro drawings, kindly answered many questions regarding the engine's development, and documented all the relevant dates. Pierre Terblanche, the creator of the Supermono and new Desmo-quattro, provided another insight into the Supermono. He was as forthcoming as possible about the new 999 design for 2003. Others at Ducati were also of assistance, particularly Livio Lodi of Museo Ducati, who also acted as interpreter; Julian Thomas and Corrado Ceccinelli of Ducati Corse; Ludovica Benedetti of the Press Department; and Daniele Casolari of Ducati Performance. Warren Lee of Norm Fraser Importers, Australia, provided current workshop manuals. For the use of motorcycle magazine archives, I am especially grateful to Brian Catterson, executive editor of *Cycle World* magazine; Jeremy Bowdler, editor of *Two Wheels* magazine; Ken Wootton, editor of *Australian Motorcycle News*; and Franco Bartoli, of *Moto Italiane*. Others who helped with information, photos, and provided access to motorcycles were Phil Aynsley, Gerolamo Bettoni, Rolf im Brahm, Jerry Dean, Leigh Farrall, Jeffrey Foord, Robert Grant, Graham Hadley, Kai Higdon, Darren Hyland, Roy Kidney, Gregg Rammell, Peter Shearman, Heinz Tschinkel, Chris Tselepatiotis, Guy Webster, and Jonathan White.

As always, I received enthusiastic support from those at MBI, in particular Darwin Holmstrom, Zack Miller, and Tim Parker. Finally I would like to thank my wife, Miriam, and sons Benjamin and Timothy for their patience while I was preparing this manuscript.

—Ian Falloon

Chapter One

851 1986–1992

When the Castiglioni brothers, Claudio and Gianfranco, purchased Ducati from the VM Group in 1985, they inherited an engine line-up based around the venerable Mille bevel-drive twin and the 350–750-cc Pantah. Ducati's tradition since 1954 was to race, and the Castiglionis wanted this to continue. Yet, while the bevel-drive engine was by then obsolete for racing, the Pantah was still achieving some success. For 1986, the Pantah was enlarged to 851 cc, and Marco Lucchinelli won the Battle of the Twins race at Daytona and Laguna Seca. All the signs indicated that the air-cooled two-valve engine wasn't dead yet. However, the Castiglionis had other ideas. They wanted a totally modern engine that would be eligible to compete in the burgeoning Superbike class, an engine that would provide a basis for future development. It needed four valves per cylinder, liquid cooling, and preferably, desmodromic valve gear.

Following the positive reception of the radical Ducati Paso at the 1985 Milan Show, Cagiva felt the time was right for Ducati to embrace four-valve technology. With Ing. Fabio Taglioni—the designer of every successful racing engine up to then—in semiretirement, Cagiva looked to Ing. Massimo Bordi to coordinate this project. Bordi had already assisted in the design of the bevel-drive Mille, coming to Ducati in 1978 with an engineering thesis on an air-cooled, four-valve desmodromic cylinder head. This was completed in 1975 under the supervision of Professor Bartolozzi and Taglioni, even though it was well known that Taglioni had a distrust of four-valve engines. The shape of the intake ports dictated that neither the 1971 Grand Prix, 500-cc bevel-drive experiment, nor a subsequent belt-drive Armaroli design of 1973 offer any improvement over existing two-valve designs. Even in 1978, Taglioni had a pair of four-valve heads cast for the 900 Super Sport but didn't get around to bench testing them. Rather than a four-valve per cylinder twin, Taglioni favored a V-four, created by placing two 500-cc Pantah engines side-by-side. Bordi, though, was more enthusiastic in accepting modern automotive technology, and was prepared to combine Cosworth's cylinder head design with Taglioni's desmodromics.

Bordi was also a particular admirer of Cosworth, an English company created by Mike Costin and Keith Duckworth, which produced some of the most successful ever Formula One car racing engines. Thus, it was to Cosworth that Bordi turned when it came to the thermodynamic design of the four-valve cylinder head, and he consulted Cosworth from September 1985 until January 1986. Cosworth offered to develop and produce a prototype nondesmodromic engine for 1.5 billion lire. Because Cosworth had

The Desmoquattro development team with the 748 prototype just prior to the Bol d'Or in September 1986. Massimo Bordi is second from the left, with Gianluigi Mengoli almost hidden behind the machine. On the far right is long-time Ducati racer and technician Franco Farnè. *Museo Ducati*

unsuccessfully experimented with desmodromics on its DFV/DFY V-8, it wouldn't commit to a desmo. Thus, Bordi considered four-valve heads with conventional valve springs, along with five valves (as with the Yamaha), or six valves (Maserati), but finally decided on a four-valve desmo. In early 1986 Gianluigi "Gigi" Mengoli began initial drawings. In his words, "I had to do this at home to avoid the fury of Taglioni, who still remained skeptical of four-valves." The first design had straight ports inclined at 30 degrees, with very close rockers and side-mounted spark plugs, but it was soon revised with a blind pin to allow space for a central spark plug. By April 13, Mengoli had finished the drawings for a compact, liquid-cooled, double-overhead camshaft four-valve desmodromic cylinder head meeting all of Bordi's requirements.

From Cosworth came the 40-degree included valve angle. This was from the F2 FVA 1,600-cc engine, but even in 1986 it was arguably obsolete. The successful 3-liter DFV Formula One engine had a 38-degree included valve angle, and the later DFY a 22-degree

angle. However, while Bordi would have preferred a narrower included valve angle, the rocker setup for the desmodromic valve gear made this impossible. Only 15 years later, with the Testastretta, would a solution be found, allowing a narrower included valve angle with desmodromic valve control. Cosworth also helped design a suitable exhaust and injection system, allowing a straight inlet manifold with a steep, 45-degree downdraft along with large 48-mm throttle bodies. For this new cylinder head, Bordi modified and adapted his earlier thesis design. Instead of the four rockers being positioned outside the camshafts, all the rockers were located between the camshafts. One feature both his thesis design and the OVD (Otto Valvole Desmo or eight valve desmo) shared was the 40-degree included valve angle. Yet, while the thesis design was air-cooled and used a bevel gear drive, the new liquid-cooled engine featured Pantah-style, toothed rubber belts to drive the double overhead camshafts. This system was initially designed by Taglioni and Bigondi using Bordi's thesis, with its horizontal intake ports as a basis. The valve sizes on the prototype were 34 mm inlet and 30 mm exhaust, and an 11.0:1 compression ratio was attained, still with a flat-topped Mondial piston with Tecnol cylinders. The con-rods were Carrillo, with the same 124-mm length as the Pantah and a 20-mm wristpin.

Central to the design was the Weber Marelli "I.A.W. Alfa/N" open-loop, fully mapped, electronic fuel injection system originally developed for the Ferrari F40 sports car and Formula One. Defined as an Alpha/N-type, alpha represented the angle at which the throttle butterfly met the incoming air and N the number of engine revs. This equated a four-stroke engine to that of an air compressor with a given volumetric efficiency and with twin injectors per cylinder and six sensors, it suited a twin cylinder motorcycle perfectly. The electronic control unit was an I.A.W. 043 (07), and this would feature on all 851s (and 888s) through until 1993. The computer used an EPROM (electronically programmable read-only memory) that contained a map of fuel and ignition requirements derived from dyno tests. Work on adapting this system to a motorcycle began in January 1986 under the leadership of Aurelia Lionello. His team at Marelli (Busi, Mezzette, and Lenzi) undoubtedly provided the impetus for the ultimate technical dominance of the OVD on the racetrack.

Using modified Pantah crankcases, (with more widely spaced cylinder studs), the prototype engine was 748 cc, so it could run in the Bol d'Or 24 Hour endurance race at Paul Ricard in the south of France on September 19, 1986. The dimensions of 88x61.5 mm came from the 750 F1, and in determining the size of the cooling system, Bordi used his earlier experience with diesel engines. A water pump was fitted on the left, running off the cam-belt drive shaft, moving the water through a 14-pass, cross-flow radiator. It wasn't the neatest arrangement, but it was indicative of the urgency in completion. In April 1986, the blueprint drawings were dispatched to the foundry and work proceeded until the engine was first started on August 30, 1986. The first time on the dyno, this produced 82.18 horsepower at 7,862 rpm, this soon rising to 94 horsepower. To speed development, the engine was placed in a modified 750 F1 frame that had been prepared during the August summer break. Early tests in a 750

Paso box-section steel frame indicated the longer front cylinder head would hit the front wheel, so frame specialist Roger Manning created a new chassis. This was a traditional, tubular-steel space frame (with 25x1.5-mm main tubing) and a braced aluminum swingarm, also featuring a linkage rising rate rear suspension similar to the final racing 750 TT1. As with the Pantah, the swingarm pivoted on the rear of the crankcases, and to reduce some of the plumbing required, the 22-mm triangular cross tube was used as coolant pipe. The bodywork had been created earlier (in July), so by September 15th, the 748 was ready for its first test at Mugello. It looked like a prototype, and was a little overweight at 376 pounds (170 kilograms), but showed incredible promise considering that it was completed in two weeks. At the Bol d'Or four days later, ridden by Marco Lucchinelli, Juan Garriga, and Virginio Ferrari, after 13 hours the 748 was in seventh place before retiring with a broken con-rod bolt.

This retirement almost saw an end to the four-valve project. At the nonchampionship Barcelona 24 Hour race in October, Juan Garriga, Carlos Cardus, and Benjamin Grau rode Lucchinelli's Daytona-winning, 851-cc two-valve Pantah to victory. It was now producing around 90 horsepower, and Taglioni wanted to concentrate on the development of

Even when it was developed as an 851, the racer wasn't a pretty motorcycle. It was very effective though, and Marco Lucchinelli rode this prototype 851 racer to victory in the Battle of the Twins race at Daytona in 1987. *Cycle World*

this design, which was still providing good results. Bordi, however, was still committed to the four-valve engine, and by early 1987 had increased this to 851 cc (92x64 mm). Immediately the four-valve proved more powerful than the two-valve, and with 115 horsepower shown on the dyno, it was the first time a Ducati engine had exceeded the 100-horsepower mark. The future of the new engine was assured, and Bordi wanted to call it the "850." However, according to Mengoli, "I wanted to avoid any association with the doomed Fiat 850 automobile, so I persuaded Bordi to call it the 851."

The 851 1987

Sensing that the Pantah crankcases would be stretched to the limit by more horsepower, Bordi and Mengoli designed new crankcases for the 851. These were stronger and larger, and allowed for a six-speed gearbox. A deeper sump provided a half-liter more oil, and the mounting bosses were now full-length across the crankcase. The

crankshaft and con-rods were highly polished, and despite the longer stroke, the con-rod length remained at 124 mm. Inside the cylinder head, the valve sizes were reduced to 32 mm for the inlet with 10 mm of valve lift, and 28 mm for the exhaust with 9 mm of lift. Along with the increase in capacity came a corresponding increase in compression (the three-ring Mondial pistons giving a 12:1 compression ratio), and there was a new gearshift arrangement. The Weber Marelli injection system was much as before, with twin injectors for each cylinder and 47-mm throttle bodies. The power (at the rear wheel) was 120 horsepower at 11,500 rpm.

Much was retained from the Bol d'Or prototype, including the frame with its 27.5-degree steering head angle. The wheelbase was a moderate 55.8 inches (1,430 mm), and the weight came down slightly to 165 kilograms. Suspension, wheels, and brakes were also similar to the 1986 748 prototype—42-mm Marzocchi M1R forks, a GSG Roma single shock absorber, and the

A prototype street version of the 851 developed during 1987 featured a racing exhaust system and braced aluminum swingarm. *Museo Ducati*

usual Brembo brakes. Up front were twin 320-mm floating front discs and four-piston racing calipers, and at the rear was a 230-mm disc.

Although it still looked unfinished with its maze of pipes and the electronic control unit crudely strapped to the side of the engine, in early March, the 851 was taken to Daytona for the Battle of the Twins race. Marco Lucchinelli, 1981 World 500-cc champion, easily won the race, but more significantly, he was timed at 165.44 miles per hour, only 6 miles per hour under Wayne Rainey's factory Honda VFR 750 Superbike. After the success at Daytona, Ducati decided to contest the 1987 Italian Superbike Trophy, pitting 1,000-cc twins against 750-cc fours. Unfortunately, the quest for horsepower and revs beyond 11,000 resulted in decreased reliability, and Lucchinelli retired several times because of electrical problems and crankshaft failure. Vibration played havoc with the electronics, and the engine would stall inexplicably. It took a complete season to isolate the problem, caused by the flywheel pick-ups failing due to extreme oil temperatures, resulting in an engine management malfunction. Marelli eventually modified the software during 1989. Thus, Lucchinelli only won two Italian Superbike races during 1987, at Monza and Misano. To prevent further crank failure, Austrian Pankl titanium con-rods (H-section, in the style of a Carrillo) with larger big-end journals (42 mm, up from 40 mm) were fitted. The valve sizes also went back to 34 and 30 mm.

As the racing program was proceeding, so too was the development of a street version, and by mid-June the first of these was tested. Without an airbox, and with megaphone exhausts, the power was around 95 horsepower at 9,000 rpm. With durability in mind, there were new Tecno Cereal cylinders. Chassis development during 1987 also saw a reduction in the steering head angle to 26 degrees. Rather than the racer's 17-inch magnesium wheels, the street prototype featured 16-inch composite Marvic/Akront wheels similar to those of the 750 F1 Montjuich and Santa Monica. This also included 280-mm front brake discs and a 260-mm rear disc. With a Ribald hand-crafted steel fairing, the weight was around 409 pounds (185 kilograms). Then in November 1987, the first production run commenced—seven 851 Superbikes, followed in January 1988 by the first series of the Superbike Kit.

To homologate the 851 for World Superbike racing in 1988, the *Tricolore* 851 Superbike Kit was produced. *Cycle World*

The 851 Superbike Kit 1988

There were always several levels of specification offered with the Desmoquattro, with the 851 Corsa (Racing) available in limited numbers for racing. The homologation model was initially the 851 Superbike Kit, and later the SP (Sport Production), while the 851 Strada (street) was the regular production model.

As Ducati was a manufacturer producing fewer than 50,000 motorcycles a year, the homologation requirements for World Superbike required 200 units of the 851 to be built for 1988. This homologation machine was known as the 851 Superbike Kit, and it was a confused mixture of racer and street bike. Here was a machine designed for racing that came with Michelin racing slick tires, but also featured an electric start, headlight, and taillight. Fortunately there were no turn signal indicators or rearview mirrors. Known as the "Tricolore" because of the distinctive red, white, and green color scheme, 207 Superbike Kits were produced; 54 going to the United States so that the 851 could be homologated for AMA Superbike racing.

The heart of the Superbike Kit was a race-kitted 851-cc engine that produced an impressive 120 horsepower at 10,000 rpm at the crankshaft. The nimonic valves were 32 and 28 mm in diameter, controlled by desmodromic "kit" camshafts. The flat-topped 92-mm piston had a 0.3-mm rise over that of the Strada, giving a compression ratio of 10.7:1. From the 1987 Superbike came Pankl con-rods, and the Superbike Kit featured a closer-ratio six-speed "kit" gearbox than the Strada. Shared with the 750 and 906 Paso was the problematic 14-plate dry clutch. The Weber Marelli electronic ignition and fuel injection system was also the same P7 system used by the racer, with twin injectors for each cylinder. This used two pick-ups. An rpm sensor was mounted opposite the flywheel to detect the four tabs on the flywheel rim, while the injection timing sensor was placed opposite the timing gear, detecting a tab on that gear. It was an

extremely effective setup and would last until the final 996 SPS of 2000. The exhaust system was a racing style, similar to that on Lucchinelli's Donington-winning 851.

Generally the chassis of the 851 Superbike Kit reflected developments from the official 1987 racing program. Still with a lazy 27.5 degree steering head angle, and 104 mm of trail, the chrome-molybdenum tubular steel frame was similar, and incorporated a braced aluminum swingarm with a rising rate linkage. The suspension was by Marzocchi, with 41.7-mm M1R forks and a Supermono rear shock absorber. While the wheels were racing Marvic 17-inch magnesium, with state-of-the-art rim widths (3.50 and 5.50 inches), for some reason, small (280-mm) cast-iron front discs were fitted. The brake calipers, though, were racing Brembo P4.32B with four, 32-mm pistons. At the rear was a surprisingly large 260-mm disc, with a Brembo P2.08N caliper.

Completing the racing specification were Michelin slick tires, a 12/60 on the front and on 18/67 on the rear.

On paper the 851 Superbike Kit looked impressive, but its main problem was excessive weight. The claim of 365 pounds (165 kilograms) was undoubtedly spurious, as that was the actual weight of the factory racer in 1987, which didn't run lights. The actual weight of the Superbike Kit was around 420 pounds (190 kilograms) dry, and this was far too much for a racer. Combined with limited information on the injection system and replacement EPROMs, the Superbike Kit was disappointing for those expecting to race as privateers in Superbike. With factory assistance, things were different. Stefano Caracchi brought a factory 851 Superbike Kit to Daytona in 1988 and finished second in the Pro-Twins race. The machine then went to

The first street version of the *Desmoquattro* was the 1988 851 Strada. This also promised much but failed to deliver. The Marvic/Akront 16-inch wheels contributed to strange handling.
Ian Falloon

Eraldo Ferracci, who developed it further; in the hands of Dale Quarterley, it won the Pro-Twins title.

The 851 Superbike (Strada) 1988

Complementing the 851 Superbike Kit was the first 851 street series, the 851 Strada. These also were limited production machines, with 304 manufactured in April 1988. The general engine specifications were similar to the 851 Superbike Kit, with 32- and 28-mm valves and Pankl con-rods. The flat-topped pistons gave a 10.2:1 compression ratio. With Strada cams and a Mototank Paso-style exhaust system, the power was 102 horsepower at 9,000 rpm at the crankshaft. The 851 Strada also had a wider ratio gearbox than the Superbike Kit but retained the twin fuel injectors per cylinder.

While the frame and suspension was shared with the Superbike Kit, the 851 Strada didn't feature the braced aluminum swingarm (although it did appear in the official brochure). There were a few changes to the running gear, particularly the wheels. From the 1987 prototype came the 16-inch Marvic/Akront composite wheels (aluminum rims with magnesium spokes). The rim sizes were 3.50-inch on the front and 5.00-inch on the rear, and they came shod with Michelin radial tires. The brakes were identical to the Superbike Kit except for street Brembo P4.32B front brake calipers. These early Stradas also had braided steel brake lines.

As it was a limited production item, many of the components were individually crafted on that first series, including the 20-liter aluminum fuel tank and rear suspension rocker linkage. Unfortunately, while the quality of execution was high, the 1988 851 Strada was a flawed motorcycle. Performance was disappointing considering the hype, and the claimed dry weight of 409 pounds (185 kilograms) was again optimistic. To rectify this, a racing modification kit was available, similar to that for the 851 Superbike Kit. The most serious problem concerned the steering and handling. The 16-inch wheels provided unsettling steering, and as a result, the 851 Strada received a lukewarm reception. Combined with an extremely high price tag, the 851 Strada was a slow-selling model. Even by the end of 1988, more than 100 were in the storeroom at the factory, prompting heavy discounting before the advent of the improved 1989 model.

World Superbike 1988–1989

Although the results in the 1987 Italian Superbike Trophy were disappointing, Bordi

While the 1989 851 Strada wasn't a limited production machine like the *Tricolore*, it was a superior motorcycle in every respect.
Ian Falloon

and his team weren't discouraged. The machine was fast enough, and only the mysterious electrical problems needed to be overcome. For 1988, Ducati decided to contest the Italian Battle of the Twins Championship, as well as the Superbike World Championship, a new series that seemed ideal for the Desmoquattro. Not only did twins receive a 250-cc capacity advantage, but their minimum weight limit was only 309 pounds (140 kilograms), compared to the fours' 365 pounds (165 kilograms). However, getting near the minimum weight was difficult, and the 1988 factory racer was only 6.6 pounds (3 kilograms) lighter than in 1987 at 358 pounds (162 kilograms).

Engine development centered on the induction and exhaust system, and with an 11.2:1 compression ratio and 33- and 29-mm valves, the power was 122 horsepower at 11,000 rpm. The throttle bodies were 50-mm and initially the capacity remained at 851 cc, with 888 cc tested and used after the Austrian round. More development occurred in the chassis, and various different swingarms were tried during the season. By the end of the year experimental 42-mm Marzocchi upside down forks were also

tested, and the steering head angle reduced one degree, to 24 degrees.

At the very first race of the new World Superbike series, held at Donington on April 3, 1988, Marco Lucchinelli rode the 851 to overall victory. Unfortunately, as had happened during 1987, continual electrical and crankshaft problems saw many retirements in subsequent races. As the power increased, there were problems with the main bearings, lubrication, and crankcases. Although Luchinelli also won the first race at Zeltweg in Austria, the Ducati team decided not to contest the final two rounds in Australia and New Zealand. In retrospect, this was a mistake, as Lucchinelli may well have taken the title if he had raced those final rounds. Still, Lucchinelli finished fifth overall in that inaugural season. In the Italian Twins Championship, Baldassare Monti won, earning him a ride in the World Superbike squad for the next season.

For 1989, Marco Lucchinelli became the team manager for the Squadra Corse Ducati team. Raymond Roche was now the number one rider, with assistance from Baldassare Monti and occasionally Massimo Broccoli and Lucchinelli himself. Roche was a former Grand Prix rider (having finished third in the

Raymond Roche rode for Marco Lucchinelli's team in the 1989 World Superbike Championship. The 888-cc racer featured an Öhlins upside down front fork. *Two Wheels*

saw the power increase to 128 horsepower. More emphasis on weight saving again proved beneficial. Weight was now down to 349 pounds (158 kilograms). The forks were upside down Öhlins, and there was a stronger swingarm. Yet, there were still too many mechanical and electrical problems, and although Roche won more races than anyone else (five) he only ended third in the championship. At some of the fastest circuits (Hockenheim and Brainerd) Roche took double victories, indicating the impressive speed of the 888. Even though Monti gave the 851 its first series victory in the Italian Superbike Championship, Ducati still needed to improve its reliability.

The 851 Strada 1989

Although no longer a limited production model (with 751 constructed), and showing obvious signs of cost cutting, the 851 Strada was significantly improved for 1989. Apart from a slight increase in the compression ratio, to 10.5:1, and a single injector per cylinder for the Weber I.A.W. 043 (07) injection system, the engine specifications were largely unchanged. There were smaller diameter intakes (27 mm from 28 mm) and 20-mm shorter inlet manifolds. Two types of cylinder head were fitted during 1989, one stamped "C1" and the other "C2." The "C2" featured modified valve seats for larger valves and cylinder heads machining for higher compression. There also was a revised 16-plate dry clutch, and a new 42-mm aluminum Termignoni exhaust system. The claimed power was increased slightly to 105 horsepower at 9,000 rpm (at the crankshaft).

The most significant change for 1989 were white-painted aluminum Brembo 17-inch wheels, front and rear, with rim sizes of 3.50 and 5.50 inches. While the frame (also painted white) was similar to before, reducing the steering head angle to 24.5 degrees and the trail to 94 mm contributed to the superior steering. Marzocchi M1R forks remained with a rear Marzocchi Duo 38 shock absorber. This unit was quite satisfactory but it was important to maintain the air pressure at 114 psi (8 kg/cm2). The front brake disc diameter was also increased to 320 mm (though these were steel and no longer the fully floating cast-iron type) and the rear disc reduced to 245 mm. Brembo four-piston P4.32A calipers gripped the front discs via a 15-mm master cylinder, with a P2.105N rear caliper with an

With its plain colors and minimal logos, the 1989 851 was one of Ducati's better styling efforts of the 1980s. *Ian Falloon*

500-cc World Championship in 1984), but also a successful endurance racer (winning the 1981 World Endurance Championship). Ducati again contested the Italian Superbike Championship, the two riders being Monti and Broccoli.

The factory bike now displaced 888 cc (through new 94-mm cylinders), and work on the combustion chamber design, now with 36- and 31-mm valves, and the exhaust system

11-mm master cylinder. Still only available as a Monoposto, the dry weight was 399 pounds (190 kilograms). Styling revisions also saw external turn signal indicators and more useable rearview mirrors.

The resulting 851 Strada finally delivered the handling and performance that was expected of such a high, technology race-bred motorcycle. Here was a twin that could match Japanese 750 fours, without disappointment. A "Sport Production" racing kit was also available which took the specification up to that of the 1989 851 Sport Production.

The 888 Corsa (Racing) 1989–1991

Sensing that the 851 Superbike Kit wasn't fulfilling its role, an official modification kit was released during 1989. This included 94-mm pistons and cylinders (giving 888 cc), larger valves (33 and 29 mm), a larger air intake and new exhaust system, along with a corresponding EPROM kit of four replacements (up to five percent richer). The compression ratio went up to 11.2:1 and the power at the crankshaft to 132 horsepower at 10,500 rpm. To improve breathing, the top of the airbox needed to be lowered 30 mm and the fuel tank raised 10 mm. Other components included a lighter (180-watt) alternator, aluminum timing pulleys, and lighter clutch and flywheel. Also included were the fastenings to fit the smaller (5-Ah) battery beside the engine rather than in the tail. New front and rear aluminum subframes positioned the ECU in front of the steering head. There also was a special light fiberglass fairing kit. Improved chassis components included 300-mm front discs, and a new rear shock absorber. Components deemed unnecessary included the electric start motor, timing belt covers, thermostat, electric fan, and the front headlight.

Some of these modification kits were factory-fitted to the 851 Superbike Kit, resulting in the red 851 Racing, or "Lucchinelli" Replica. However, even with this modification kit, the 851 Superbike Kit failed to deliver in the hands of privateers. This led to the first official over-the-counter 851 Corsa in 1990, also known as the Roche Replica, and 20 were produced. Apart from developments aimed at improving reliability, the engine was much as it had been with the 1989 modification kit. There was a new inlet

Although "Lucchinelli replicas" were unofficially available from 1989, the first "over-the-counter" factory race replica was produced in 1990. For 1991 there was this updated "Roche replica" 888 Corsa. *Museo Ducati*

camshaft, providing 11 mm of valve lift, along with a modified airbox, special gearbox, and a magnesium clutch cover. The clutch was specifically designed for racing and included 18 plates. Chassis improvements saw Öhlins upside down front forks and 320-mm front disc brakes. At the rear was a 210-mm disc, and the weight was a claimed 349 pounds (158 kilograms).

Following the success of the factory bike during 1990, Ducati produced 50 examples of the 851 Racing for 1991. Most of the engine specifications were as before, but the compression ratio of the 888-cc engine was up to 12:1. The valve sizes remained at 34 and 30 mm, the inlet ports at 29 mm, and the gearbox at that of the SP. Because the ratios were too wide for many tracks, a closer-ratio gearbox became available during 1991. There also was a new 20-plate clutch.

Although producing a claimed 128 horsepower at 11,000 rpm, the 1991 851 Corsa was still quite removed from the official factory machines. Chassis developments included wider wheels (a 3.75x17-inch and 6.00x17-inch), Brembo P4 30–34 front brake calipers, and a number of carbon-fiber body parts. This saw the weight reduced to 343 pounds (155 kilograms).

The 851 Strada 1990

With the 1989 Strada being more successful than the overpriced 1988 Tricolore, production was increased significantly for 1990. For this model year, 1,366 were produced, and apart from the provision for a dual seat, there were few changes from the 1989 model. The engine specifications were also similar, although the Pankl H-section steel con-rods were replaced

For 1990, the 851 Strada received a dual seat but was otherwise similar to the 1989 version.
Ian Falloon

by solid Macchi forged con-rods. Because these were not as strong or light as the Pankl, the safe maximum revs was reduced from 10,500 to 9,500 rpm. The provision of a dual seat with a stronger rear subframe saw the dry weight increase to 424 pounds (192 kilograms). Functionally though, the 1990 851 Strada performed similarly to that of 1989, with slightly less stable handling due to the altered weight distribution.

World Superbike 1990

After the impressive showing during 1989, it was inevitable that Raymond Roche and the Ducati 888 would be even more of a force during 1990. Not only was the 888 as fast, if not faster, as the four-cylinder competition, but the weight advantage would become even more apparent. Development centered on improving reliability, and with the earlier electronic problems overcome, the lubrication system and crankcases were now the primary areas of weakness. New injector trumpets improved airflow, and with even higher compression (12:1), 37-mm inlet valves, and new camshafts, the power was now 130 horsepower at 11,000 rpm, at the

rear wheel. Later in the year, a 95.6-mm bore was tried (giving 920 cc) at faster tracks, still the 888-cc version was considered more tractable. Revisions to the cooling system saw a smaller, single curved radiator, that would raise the temperature to around 158–167 degrees Fahrenheit (70–75 degrees Celsius) after it was found that the engine had been running too cool during 1989 at 104 degrees F or 40 degrees C. Crankcase problems persisted however (notably at Hockenheim), and there was difficulty finding suitable gearbox ratios. Roche had a choice of three engine and gearbox combinations for each track.

Although the chassis with Öhlins suspension was much as before, the rear section was stiffened with two additional struts, and the ride height lowered. This also had the effect of increasing the steering head angle. After starting the season at 347 pounds (157 kilograms), the weight was gradually reduced to 332 pounds (150 kilograms) but Roche was still unhappy with the long-wheelbase 888. Even during 1990, he was calling for a shorter engine and a new frame, and in early 1990 there were rumors

Consistent development reduced the weight of Raymond Roche's 1990 World Superbike 888 to 332 pounds (150 kilograms), but reliability was still questionable. *Two Wheels*

of the new, single-sided swingarm, Tamburini-designed frame making an appearance at the Suzuka 8-Hour race. A new *evoluzione* machine did appear at Monza, with carbon-fiber mufflers, tank, and fairing. There was new LCD instrumentation, and the CPU was moved from under the tailpiece to in front of the steering head. These developments saw the weight decrease to 325 pounds (147 kilograms).

Roche's teammate for 1990 was Giancarlo Falappa, who had impressed everyone on the Bimota during 1989. However, not only was Roche sometimes unhappy with the motorcycle, there was occasional friction between the two riders. Falappa often crashed, suffering serious injuries at the Osterreichring practice, prematurely ending his season. Jamie

James also rode the Fast by Ferracci 851 (an upgraded 1989 model) in Canada and the United States, gaining an impressive two second places at Mosport. These performances saw him on Falappa's bike for Sugo, Le Mans, and Monza.

Roche dominated the 1990 season from the outset. After winning the two opening races at Jerez, he didn't look back, and with eight victories, easily took the championship. Falappa won one race (at Donington) but as Roche rode several races without a supporting rider, Ducati lost the Manufacturers World Championship by six points to Honda.

In the Italian Superbike Championship Davide Tardozzi and Mauro Mastrelli rode 888s sponsored by Pietro di Gianesin's Bike

2000, with Massimo Broccoli on another entry. This year they couldn't repeat the result of 1989, but on the other side of the Atlantic Jamie James took his FBF 851 to victory in the AMA Pro-Twins Championship.

The 851 Sport Production 1989–1991

Ducati built 110 851 Sport Production models for the 1989 Italian Sport Production series that pitted production 750-cc fours against twins of up to 1,000 cc. These were virtually indistinguishable from the Strada. Unlike the official racers, the capacity wasn't 888 cc, but still 851 cc. As a 1-mm overbore was allowed under the regulations, 93-mm pistons were also available, providing 869.4 cc. The compression ratio was up to 11.5:1, and the camshafts were from the earlier 851 Superbike Kit. From the racing uprating kit came 33- and 29-mm valves and a 42-mm exhaust. There was only a single injector per cylinder, but the fuel pressure was increased to 72.5 psi (5 bar), and three different EPROMs were available. There was also an external oil cooler, and with the top of the airbox removed the power was 122 horsepower at 10,000 rpm (at the crankshaft). The 851 SP chassis was pure Strada for 1989, including the Marzocchi suspension and 320-mm stainless steel front discs, but the weight was down to a claimed 398 pounds (180 kilograms).

Because the 1989 851 Sport Production wasn't as successful as expected, the SP was considerably upgraded for 1990. Although still titled an 851, the 851 SP2 displaced 888 cc through larger (94-mm) pistons. There was a return to twin injectors per cylinder (still with the 07 control unit), and the SP retained the H-section Pankl rods along with a new crankshaft with 15-tooth spline for the alternator. A 300-watt alternator accompanied this. Other upgraded components included new timing pulleys and a closer ratio gearbox with revised ratios for third, fourth, fifth, and sixth gears. The valve sizes were 33 and 29 mm with 28-mm inlet ports, and the dry clutch had a vented cover. With a 10.7:1 compression ratio, and a 45-mm Termignoni exhaust system, the power was 109 horsepower at 10,000–10,500 rpm, at the rear wheel.

One of the most spectacular production Ducatis was the 851 SP2. In 1990 this offered unparalleled street performance. *Cycle World*

Chassis improvements included upside-down 42-mm Öhlins FG 9050 front forks, an Öhlins DU 8070 shock absorber, and fully floating 320-mm Brembo cast-iron front disc brakes with higher specification Brembo P4.32d calipers. The Öhlins forks came straight from the racer and proved unsuitable for street use, with many complaints regarding leaking seals. This continued for the 1991 SP3 and resulted in Öhlins providing a free modification in late 1991. There was also an aluminum rear subframe, but the weight climbed to 415 pounds (188 kilograms), largely due to the heavier forks. Although 380 851 SP2s were produced, it was still a limited production machine providing unparalleled handling and performance in 1990.

There was a similar 851 SP3 for 1991 (also 888 cc), the most identifiable difference being the louder and more upswept

Termignoni exhaust pipes. These were homologation exhausts for the factory racers and along with larger valves (33 and 29 mm) and 0.3-mm higher pistons (giving an 11:1 compression ratio), resulted in a small power increase to 111 horsepower at 10,500 rpm (or 128 horsepower at the crankshaft). Another feature contributing to the improved performance was a forced air intake and no top on the airbox. Following the problems in World Superbike during 1990 there were stronger crankcases. There was also a new 18-plate clutch, another fastening for the alternator rotor, and a revised type of timing belt pulley. The new clutch would be featured on all later Sport Production 888s.

While the 851 SP3 continued with the same Öhlins FG 9050 forks, there was a slightly different Öhlins DU 0060 rear shock absorber. The Brembo wheels were painted black, and the front brake master cylinder increased in size to 16 mm. Both the brake and clutch master cylinders featured remotely mounted fluid reservoirs. As with the 1991 851 Strada, a degasser was incorporated in the fuel tank, resulting in a smaller capacity. There was also a new carbon-fiber front fender, homologated for World Superbike. In all other respects, the 851 SP3 was identical to the SP2, and 534 were manufactured, each receiving a numbered plaque. A small number of 851 Sport Production Specials (16) were produced for 1991, and these had an even higher performance engine (Corsa specification) and more carbon-fiber.

The 851 Strada 1991

After two years with little change, the 851 Strada received significant suspension development for 1991. Production stabilized at 1,200 bikes for the 1991 model year. The general engine specifications for the 1991 851 Strada were the same as the 1990 version. This included single fuel injectors per cylinder, Strada camshafts, and 32- and 28-

mm valves; the power was 91 horsepower at 9,000 rpm at the rear wheel. Although still with the forged Macchi con-rods, the crankshaft was now standardized with the 851 SP, with a 15-tooth spline (rather than 6-tooth) for the flywheel and alternator. This also saw the 300-watt alternator from the SP instead of the earlier 350-watt alternator. While fitted in the interest of lightness, the new alternator made the motorcycle less suitable in traffic, as the battery recharge was insufficient under 2,700 rpm with the headlight on.

While the Marzocchi M1R forks had proved satisfactory for street use, in line with current racing developments, the 1991 851 Strada featured upside down 41-mm Showa GD 011 forks. With these forks, the trail increased marginally to 95 mm, and the travel increased to 120 mm from 100 mm. An Öhlins DU 0060 shock absorber came from the 851 SP3, although there was now no longer provision for ride height adjustment. The rest of the chassis was as before, but

High-rise exhaust pipes and a carbon-fiber front fender distinguished the 1991 SP3 from the SP2. *Ian Falloon*

New for the 1991 851 Strada were Showa upside down forks. *Australian Motorcycle News*

the front brake master cylinder was increased to 16 mm, with a remote fluid reservoir. The Brembo brake calipers were still P4.32A.

Leaking clutch master cylinders in earlier 851s prompted an additional sealing O-ring for the piston, along with a remote fluid reservoir. Problems with the earlier fuel tank breather saw a larger air breather valve, and a new locking fuel cap. To overcome fuel vaporization at high temperatures, a fuel degasser was installed between the feedback valve and fuel pump. This reduced the capacity of the aluminum fuel tank to 17 liters. Styling considerations included a smaller front fender and reshaped color-matched rearview mirrors, although functionally these offered no improvement. The riding position was altered more significantly, with an increase in seat height and footpeg height. The weight was up to 440 pounds (199 kilograms).

World Superbike 1991

The *evoluzione* 888 that appeared at the final European World Superbike race at Monza in 1990 was a harbinger of things to come. With even more attention paid to weight saving, the factory 888 for 1991 weighed only 316 pounds (143 kilograms), further accentuating the weight difference

between twins and fours. Engine development continued to be centered around improving reliability, and new crankcases were built out of a higher grade of aluminum from Alcan in Canada. The design was improved with altered reinforcing. Because of its association with Formula 1, the small British company Omega now provided the 13:1 pistons, with Mondial now supplying the cylinders. To overcome some failures due to lack of oil to the wrist pin, the Pankl con-rods now featured an oil way drilled up the shaft to the little end. Lubrication was further improved by lowering the oil pump pickup. The valve sizes were 36 and 31 mm, and more attention was paid to reducing internal friction. The camshafts were unchanged, but there was a new exhaust system, a crossover type without the usual "star." There was some development to the airbox and induction chamber, with the inlet ports increased to 30 mm, although the power of the 888-cc engine was only increased marginally to 133 horsepower at 11,500 rpm.

Most of the weight saving came from extensive use of carbon-fiber for many brackets and components, along with a reduction in the rear disc size to 190 mm, from 216 mm. The factory bikes of Roche and Falappa also featured a steel/carbon front disc combination and new type Öhlins front fork. To improve the aerodynamics, new bodywork was developed in the Pininfarina wind tunnel. This included a new front fender, higher mounted silencers, and a rear fender running underneath the swingarm. The result was a five percent improvement in wind penetration. Another benefit from the altered position of various components was an improvement in weight distribution to 51/49 percent.

With Falappa still recovering from the horrendous crash of 1990, Doug Polen and Stéphane Mertens received factory 888s. Thus, Ducati was well placed to repeat the 1990 result in the World Superbike

Championship. However, the dominance of Polen on the Fast by Ferracci machine took everyone by surprise. After Polen set pole position at Daytona in 1991—unfortunately breaking a chain on the start line—Ferracci decided to attempt the World Superbike Championship. With assistance from the veteran tuners Giorgio Nepoti and Rino Caracchi of NCR, Polen (on Dunlop tires) won 17 of the 26 races that season. Not even Carl Fogarty could repeat the dominance of Polen during that 1991 season. Roche (on Michelin tires) won four races, and Mertens (on Pirelli tires) two races. Beaten only once, by Kevin Magee at Phillip Island, this year Ducati convincingly took out the

Doug Polen on the Fast by Ferracci 888 was virtually unbeatable in the 1991 World Superbike Championship. The bike weighed just 316 pounds (143 kilograms) and reliability was significantly improved. *Australian Motorcycle News*

Doug Polen, born in Detroit in 1960, set a record of seven consecutive World Superbike race wins and 10 pole positions in a season that still remains. *Australian Motorcycle News*

says Terblanche. This would be the final 851 before the series became the 888, although for 1992, the Sport Production was officially an 888 and shared the same revised styling.

In order to increase the power slightly, the new cylinder heads were shared with the 851 Sport Production while retaining the 92-mm bore and 851 cc. The valve sizes were 33 and 29 mm, although the camshafts were still Strada. Also retained from the earlier Strada were the Macchi con-rods and wider ratio gearbox. New was a curved radiator and redesigned cooling system, a forced air intake, and a return to the 350-watt alternator. To overcome flywheel loosening problems, there were now seven fasteners rather than five. These were stronger than before. Still with a single fuel injector per cylinder, the power was increased moderately to 95 horsepower at 9,000 rpm.

Changes to the white-painted frame saw single bent outer frame tubes rather than individually welded sections. The footpeg brackets were also revised. Although the upside down Showa forks were unchanged the trail was back to 94 mm. There was now also a Showa GD 012-007-0A rear shock absorber instead of the Öhlins. Modifications to the braking system saw Brembo Gold Series P4.30–34 front brake calipers, with a gold P2.105N on the rear. The Brembo wheels were painted black, and the rear suspension rod, yellow.

If the engine and chassis were much as before, Terblanche's bodywork was quite different, especially the steel (rather than aluminum) 19-liter fuel tank. This now pivoted to improve accessibility to the throttle and injection assembly. A restyled seat unit and new front fender accompanied the tank, and there were recess mounted handles for the passenger. This facelift was undoubtedly successful and the final 851 (and 888) were among the most attractive of the Desmoquattro series. As always though, with all these developments came more weight, which was now up to 446 pounds (202 kilograms). While production was still relatively high with 1,402 motorcycles manufactured, the 851 Strada now needed more displacement to remain at the forefront of sporting street motorcycles.

Manufacturers Championship. To complete the domination of the 888 in 1991, Tardozzi won the European Superbike Championship. A special endurance 888 was also prepared during 1991, but it proved unreliable.

The 851 Strada 1992

By 1992 the 851 Strada was beginning to look slow and a little dated. Tamburini's new replacement was almost complete, so the 851 was given a quick facelift to provide a more up-to-date appearance. Pierre Terblanche had joined the Cagiva Research Center during 1989, and his first solo project was this update. "They gave this to me during 1991, and I completed it in three to four weeks. At that stage we were still in Rimini,"

Chapter Two

888 1992–1994

Although the capacity had already grown to 888 cc in the Racing versions and Sport Production, Ducati continued with the 851 designation until 1992. Ducati also built a higher performance SPS (Sport Production Special), providing four levels of specification; Corsa, SPS, SP, and Strada. By 1993, the SPS had gone, but, there was a specific U.S. SPO (Sport Production Omologato) with an 888 Strada powerplant. Even with the release of the 916 for 1994, the 888 continued as Strada and SPO, while the Corsa was also an 888 with a 926-cc motor.

The 888 Strada 1993

As the official factory racers and the Sport Production series were already displacing 888 cc, it was inevitable that the production Superbike Strada would follow suit. At the same time, the series became a generic "888" rather than "851." After displacing 888 cc since 1990 but still titled 851s, in 1992 the SPS and SP4 were finally "888s," as was the Strada from 1993. These also featured Pierre Terblanche's styling facelift, completed during 1991.

The European specification 888 Strada was very similar to that of the 1992 851 Strada, and except for an 888-cc engine, most of the other specifications were shared. The 94x64-mm engine included the same valve sizes, Strada camshafts and gearbox, and single fuel injector per cylinder. There was a new front feed airbox, and because of the larger capacity and slightly higher 11:1 compression ratio, there was a moderate power increase to 100 horsepower at 9,000 rpm. One of the more important developments was to the Weber Marelli EFI. After serial number 000508, the electronic fuel injection system incorporated an updated I.A.W. 435 (P8) central processing unit instead of the 043 (07). This included a modification to prevent failure of the freewheel starter bearing during the engine stop phase, which had been a problem on earlier 851s. Unlike the Sport Production series, the 888 Strada also retained the 350-watt alternator. With an identical Biposto chassis to the 1992 851, (Showa suspension and black-painted Brembo wheels) the weight was unchanged at 202 kilograms. To set the 1993 versions apart, there were new gold "DUCATI" decals, and the red paintwork was a slightly lighter color. After five years of development, the 888 Strada not only provided slightly improved performance over the 851, but was generally a more sophisticated and civilized machine. Not surprisingly, demand was still strong, and 1,280 were manufactured for the 1993 model year.

The front profile of the 888 was similar to that of the 851, but the riding experience was superior. This is a U.S.-only 1993 888 SPO. *Ian Falloon*

For the 1993 model year, the base Desmoquattro also became an 888. Although very similar to the 1992 851 Strada, the 888 was a more refined machine. European versions like this received a dual seat. *Two Wheels*

World Superbike 1992

After winning the World Superbike Championship in 1991 on the Fast by Ferracci Ducati 888, Doug Polen was elevated to the official factory team. The imprisonment of a disgraced Marco Lucchinelli on drug charges saw another former 500 cc World Champion, Franco Uncini, as team manager. Uncini brought with him sponsorship from the Italian sunglass manufacturer Police, and signed Giancarlo Falappa to partner Polen. Polen also insisted that Eraldo Ferracci come along

as technical manager. Roche declined an offer to be part of Uncini's team, deciding instead to race a factory-supplied bike as a privateer. Ace tuner, Rolando Simonetti, prepared his machine. Stéphane Mertens, Davide Tardozzi, and Spanish rider Daniel Amatriain received factory equipment and 50 factory racing engines were prepared during the year.

Although the power of the 888-cc engine was only increased marginally to 135 horsepower at 11,200 rpm, the emphasis

was on a smoother power delivery. Significantly, the engine produced 109 horsepower at only 8,000 rpm. The valves were 36 and 31 mm, and a new exhaust camshaft and stainless-steel exhaust system allowed the engine to rev to 12,000 rpm. A still-air box was formed by the underside of the fuel tank and sealed by a carbon-fiber shroud. The intakes were 54 mm this year, and Simonetti developed a variable length inlet bellmouth for Roche, with a small power-valve-like motor. Along with a new clutch, one of the most important developments during the year was experimentation with double mapping, whereby each cylinder received its

individual computer and EPROM. Weight saving extended to a narrower crankpin, 6 mm rather than 10 mm, wide gears, hollow camshafts, and smaller crank flywheels.

The chassis was a development of the 1991 Corsa rather than the new 1992 888 style. Thus, the racing frame featured individually welded top tubes and the earlier type of footpeg brackets. The carbon-fiber bodywork also was patterned on the 1991 851 and not Terblanche's 1992 model. All machines ran updated 42-mm Öhlins forks. Polen generally used U.S.-made C-CAT carbon brake discs while Falappa ran Brembo. All the attention to weight saving

Although not as dominant on the factory 888 in 1992 as he was in 1991, Doug Polen still won the World Superbike Championship. *Australian Motorcycle News*

Polen's 1992 888 racer undressed. It was still based on the 1991 SP3, and considerable effort went into reducing the weight to only 309 pounds (140 kilograms). *Australian Motorcycle News*

and distribution saw the weight now right on the minimum 309 pounds (140 kilograms) with 52/48 percent front to rear weight distribution. It was no wonder that the four-cylinder competition was complaining about the inequitable weight regulations.

Without any extensive off-season testing, and with new components being tested on the track in the early races, Polen had a slow start to the season. It wasn't until he reverted to his 1991 setup that he finally took a double win at Hockenheim. In the meantime, Roche won at Albacete and Donington, and Carl Fogarty took a victory at Donington on an 888 Corsa. Polen no longer had exclusive use of the best Dunlop tires, Falappa also used Dunlop this year, though Roche remained with Michelin. Roche's 888 was often the fastest and took him to six victories during the year, but he was penalized for his slow starts. Ultimately Polen took the title again, winning nine of the 26 races, with able assistance from a

revitalized Falappa who won four races. Falappa's double win in Austria, at the same circuit where he nearly lost his life in 1990, showed extraordinary courage. However, while the 888 was still dominant, it was coming under increased competition from the improved Yamaha and Kawasaki.

The 888 SPO
(Sport Production Omologato)

Although not featuring in official Ducati promotional literature outside the United States, for the U.S. market, the 888 was sold as the 888 SPO. This was an amalgam of the limited production high performance SP5, and the European-specification 888 Strada. Because the raucous SP5 was unable to pass strict U.S. DOT requirements, the SPO was created to homologate the 888 for AMA Superbike competition. However, though they were titled as Sport Production, they were more closely related to the 888 Strada than the SP5.

Apart from a different EPROM, the engine of the SPO was identical to that of the 888 Strada. With 100 horsepower, this had a single fuel injector per cylinder, and there was no external oil cooler. When it came to the chassis though, the SPO shared more with the higher specification SP5. While the stainless steel front discs were from the Strada, as were the lower specification Showa GD 011 forks, the SPO had the single seat, upswept exhaust pipes (without carbon-fiber mufflers), and an Öhlins DU 8071 shock absorber (along with eccentric ride height adjustment). Even though it was a Monoposto, there wasn't an aluminum rear subframe, and there was a conspicuous lack of weight-saving carbon-fiber. The front fender was from the 888 Strada, as were the black-painted Brembo wheels, but the claimed weight of 415 pounds (188 kilograms) was the same as the SP5.

Compared with other versions of the 888, only a small number of SPOs were produced. For the 1993 model year, these numbered only 170, plus an additional 120 equipped to meet the California

specifications. Even though the 916 had been released, a further 100 SPOs were produced in January 1994 (25 for California and 75 for the rest of the United States), with only detail changes from 1993. Alterations included a carbon-fiber front fender, bronze frame-matching wheels, a larger diameter front axle, and a numbered plaque on the top triple clamp.

The 888 Corsa (Racing) 1992–1994

As usual, there was an official cataloged racing 888 for 1992. Like the factory racers that year, it was based on the 1991 SP3 rather than the 1992 SP4. Thus, it retained the earlier frame, as well as the previous tank and seat styling. The engine was very similar to that of the 1991 Corsa, but for a new exhaust camshaft and Termignoni exhaust system to widen the powerband. The valves remained at 34 and 30 mm, and there was still 128 horsepower at 11,000 rpm.

More attention was paid to weight saving, and there was a new carbon-fiber and Kevlar fuel tank with a quick release and safety valve. Additional carbon-fiber components

Like the 888 Sport Production, the 888 SPO was a Monoposto only with upswept exhausts, but the engine specifications were the same as the 888 Strada.
Ian Falloon

such as footpeg brackets saw the weight down to 332 pounds (150 kilograms), although this was still noticeably heavier than the official factory racers. However, for the first time, a production Corsa was able to beat the factory machines, when Carl Fogarty won at Donington. Fewer 888 Corsas were produced in 1992 than in 1991. Ducati built 30 for 1992, and built just one during 1993. Three 1992 specification machines were also produced in 1994, plus one more in 1995.

The 888 Racing for 1993 shared the newly homologated frame and bodywork with the factory bikes, and through the use of more carbon-fiber, the weight was down to 320 pounds (145 kilograms). While still 888 cc, larger valve sizes of 36 mm and 31 mm, a new exhaust camshaft (with 10.5 mm of valve lift), and a new airbox raised the power to 135 horsepower at 11,500 rpm, at the rear wheel. The airbox was larger and now used the frame tubes to optimize the shape of the intakes. The pistons were Mondial, and

with a chrome-molybdenum Pankl con-rod, weighed 14 ounces (400 grams). There was a revised combustion chamber design for lower lead content fuel. There was also a closer ratio six-speed gearbox with the first four gears raised considerably, an improved clutch, and differential mapping for the two cylinders. The Brembo brakes and Marchesini wheels were much as before, but there was evolutionary Öhlins suspension. Forty-six 888 Racing machines were manufactured for 1993.

Although the factory raced the new 916 during 1994, the consumer 888 Racing was much the same as the 1993 926-cc factory racer. Displacing 926 cc, the 888 Racing engine featured 37-mm and 31-mm nimonic valves, 96-mm 12:1 Omega pistons, titanium con-rods, and an improved crankcase design to combat breakage. There was also a new gear selector mechanism and a new oil bleed. With specific attention aimed at reducing reciprocating weight, 5.6 ounces (160 grams) was saved through using the Omega pistons and titanium con-rods. The entire crankshaft assembly was also lighter by 28 ounces or 800 grams, and with a larger 48-mm exhaust system, the engine produced 142 horsepower at 11,500 rpm. The CPU was now an I.A.W. 435 (P8). The frame was altered too, with the steering head angle at 22.5 degrees. Other changes included a new airbox; revised 42-mm Öhlins front fork, shock absorber, and steering damper; a new crankcase breather and tank; and five-spoke Marchesini wheels, with rim sizes of 3.50x17 and 6.00x17. There was a mercury switch in case of a fall, new narrow-faced front disc rotors, a thinner rear disc, a revised rear brake antihop device, and new Michelin racing tires. Only 32 of the 888 Racing machines were

produced for 1994, as they were effectively superseded by the new 916. However, there were many initial problems with setting up the 916 for racing, and the tried and tested 888/926 was still an impressive performer in Superbike racing.

The 888 Sport Production 1992–1993

For 1992, there were two officially listed 888 Sport Production models, the SP4 and SPS (Sport Production Special). Sharing Terblanche's new style bodywork of the 1992 851 Strada, they both had a solo seat, and while the SP4 retained the specifications of the earlier SP3, the SPS provided even higher performance.

But for the revised cooling system and curved radiator, a new front feed airbox, and a small increase in the compression ratio (to 11.2:1) through 0.3-mm higher pistons, the

While providing almost identical performance to the 851 SP3, the 888 SP4 featured new styling and decals. *Ian Falloon*

engine for the 888 SP4 was the same as that
of the SP3. It was also rated at 111
horsepower at 10,500 rpm. The SPS engine
had an even higher specification than the
SP4. The valves were increased to 34 and 30
mm, with the inlet camshaft of the 888
Corsa. This opened the inlet valve 11 mm, as
opposed to 10 mm on the SP4. Along with
this higher performance cylinder head came
higher compression pistons. At 2 mm higher,
the 11.48-ounce (328-gram) pistons provided
a compression ratio of 11.7:1.

There were few changes to the
crankshaft, but the 16.8-ounce (480-gram)
888 SPS Pankl con-rods were straight from
the Corsa and incorporated the additional oil
way to the little end. The SPS also used the
twin injector Weber Marelli EFI of the Corsa,
along with a Termignoni racing exhaust
system with carbon-fiber mufflers, to give
120 horsepower at 10,500 rpm. The cooling

system also was from the Corsa, with a
lightweight curved radiator and no electric
fan. During the production run of the SP4
and SPS there was a clutch modification to
improve clutch release. Although still with
18 plates, the 3.5-mm driving plate was
eliminated. The SPS also received a
cut-away racing-vented aluminum
clutch cover.

The 888 SP4 and SPS both featured the
new frame of the 1992 851 Strada, which
had revised footpeg mounts and bent outer
tubes. As with the SP3, there was an
aluminum rear subframe, and the same
Öhlins upside-down fork and shock absorber.
For the SP4 and SPS there was an official
recall to replace the oil seals on the Öhlins
forks in early 1992. The only difference
to the braking system from the SP3 was new
Brembo brake calipers, with two P4.30–34
Gold Series calipers on the front.

From the 1992 851 Strada came the pivoting restyled fuel tank, made of steel on the 888 SP4 and quick release carbon-fiber (with a carbon-fiber tank cap) on the 888 SPS. This contributed to the reduction in weight for the SPS to 409 pounds (185 kilograms), as opposed to the 414 pounds (188 kilograms) of the SP4. There continued to be numbered plaques on both 888 SPs sharing the same sequence and although 500 SP4s were manufactured, the 888 SPS was a very limited production machine and only 101 were produced. It was also undeniably the most exotic production street motorcycle available in 1992, providing performance that is still impressive a decade later.

The final 888 Sport Production was the 888 SP5 of 1993. With the higher performance SPS engine—but with an SP4 cooling system and 118 horsepower at 10,500 rpm—this continued to set the performance standard for twin-cylinder motorcycles. There was a newer I.A.W. 435 (P8) CPU, and the engine still featured twin injectors. The SP5 also included a standard noise reducing clutch cover but retained all the usual SPS features, such as the Corsa inlet camshaft, racing Pankl con-rods, and close-ratio gearbox.

Giancarlo Falappa was one of the most spectacular Ducati Superbike riders, but his career was dogged by injury. In 1993 he rode alongside Carl Fogarty in Raymond Roche's team. *Ian Falloon*

When it came to the chassis, there were a few differences. The frame and wheels were painted bronze, and Showa GD 061 forks replaced the expensive but troublesome Öhlins forks, though an Öhlins DU 8071 shock was retained on the rear. The SP5 also featured Termignoni carbon-fiber mufflers and a fully floating rear disc brake. The brake lines were now braided steel, and, as with the SP4, 500 examples were manufactured. Also available for the SP5 was an even louder competition exhaust system, which included a replacement EPROM (040B).

Although there have been continual Sport Production series of the 916 and 996, the 888 SPs represent a different era for Ducati. These machines were loud, hard-edged race replicas, offering considerably more performance than an 851 or 888 Strada. They also were built in fewer numbers than

later SPs, and their rarity has resulted in diminished appreciation of their qualities.

World Superbike 1993

With Honda delaying the release of its new fuel-injected RC45 until the 1994 season, the 888 soldiered on for another year, giving it seven years of competition life. This was later only matched by the 916/996, but despite its age, the 888 was still the machine to beat. With nothing left to prove in Europe, Doug Polen headed back to the United States to compete in the AMA Superbike Championship, while Roche retired from racing to assume the position of team manager. Rolando Simonetti came with Roche as chief mechanic. Joining Falappa in the factory team was Carl Fogarty, with factory support also going to the Team Grottini operation managed by Davide Tardozzi.

Grottini's riders were Juan Garriga and Stéphane Mertens, with the machines tuned by Pietro di Gianesin. Mauro Lucchiari had started the season on a private Corsa, but excellent results saw him receive factory support.

Although the engine started out with only a few improvements over the 1992 title winner, the speed of Scott Russell's Kawasaki prompted the release of a 96x64-mm (926-cc) engine for faster circuits. For the first time there was a fuel restriction, with Avgas 100 being the required standard, and with 37- and 31-mm valves, and an 11.9:1 compression ratio, the power was up to around 144 horsepower at 11,500 rpm. However the engine wasn't as responsive as the 138-horsepower 888 that was still used on tighter tracks. Another problem was excessive blow-by from the Omega pistons, requiring a second crankcase breather. Thus the 926-cc engine was nicknamed "Il Pompone," or literally, big pump. To counteract rear wheel chatter, there was also a Sprague-type antilock clutch, and to improve engine pickup, titanium Pankl con-rods were used, along with considerabe internal engine lightening. Double mapping was now used exclusively, and there was a new stainless steel spaghetti-shaped exhaust system. The airbox was a one-piece sealed unit instead of the three-piece design of 1992, with the variable length intakes that Simonetti developed for Roche during 1992. Simonetti also developed an electronic quick shifter and experimented with an early form of EPROM monitoring through a series of display modules on the dashboard.

With the new SP4 bodywork and frame homologated from July 1992, the factory racers benefited from the slightly improved aerodynamics of this design, even though the frame modifications were cosmetic. There was a new swingarm to accommodate a wider (6.25-inch) rear wheel, and as the weight regulations required twins to weigh 320 pounds (145 kilograms) some components were stronger and heavier—noticeably the lower triple clamp. The 42-mm Öhlins fork and shock absorber were also improved over the previous year, and the front brakes generally were 290-mm Brembo carbon. In wet conditions, 320-mm steel discs were still used, and sometimes a cocktail of both types. A higher ride height was used to steepen the effective steering-head angle.

With 19 wins spread between Fogarty, Falappa, and privateer Andreas Meklau, Ducati still won the constructor's championship, although the rider's title went to Kawasaki's Scott Russell. Both Fogarty and Falappa were dogged by bad luck, and Fogarty won more races, 11, than any other rider, but there were too many factory-supported machines for the racing department to cope with. At the same time, resources were being utilized in the development of the new 916. The most surprising result was Meklau's victory at Zeltweg. With a 926-cc engine developed by his tuner, Edgar Schnyder, Meklau beat all of the factory machines.

Even when the 888 Strada was released for 1993, the much-rumored 916 was waiting to be released. It was the continued dominance of the 888 in the World Superbike Championship that saw the 916 release delayed until the end of 1993. Thus, the 888 Strada continued for another year, and because this was really an interim model, there were few changes. From the middle of 1993, all models were fitted with new Brembo P4 30–34C front brake calipers to reduce the front brake lever stroke. Battery charging problems also saw thicker PVC alternator cables. The 1994 888 Stradas featured bronze-painted wheels and instrument panel support, a larger diameter front axle (20 mm rather than 17 mm) and black anodized foot controls and footpegs. There also were braided steel front brake lines. Although most of the 1,200 were produced toward the end of 1993, 300 were manufactured in 1994.

AMA Superbike 1992–1994

After his impressive dominance of the 1991 World Superbike Championship, Doug Polen announced he would try to win two titles for 1992: the AMA Superbike National Championship in addition to World Superbike. Although he rode for the official factory team in World Superbike, Polen remained with Ferracci for the AMA series, joined by Pascal Picotte. After a stunning opening race at Daytona where Kawasaki-mounted Scott Russell beat Polen by a scant 0.182 seconds, Polen then won three races out of the seven he competed in. Although he missed two events due to World Superbike commitments, Polen still finished third in the championship.

For 1993 Polen decided not to defend the World Superbike crown but to endeavor to

win his first AMA Superbike National Championship. This he did in impressive style, winning 6 of the 10 rounds. Polen's 1993 Fast by Ferracci 888 was a 1992 specification machine, now producing 142 horsepower. Unlike World Superbike regulations, the weight for twins in AMA Superbike that year was still 309 pounds (140 kilograms), and with Polen on board this was a considerable advantage.

After winning both World and AMA Superbike Championships, Polen sought other fields; Australian Superbike Champion Troy Corser took his place in the Ferracci team. Although the AMA racer was based on a 926 Corsa, Eraldo Ferracci installed a longer (66-mm) stroke crankshaft from a 916. This gave a displacement of 955 cc, and with around 155 horsepower made even more power than the factory 916 955-cc racers, because of a freer flowing exhaust allowed by the 888 chassis. It was also advantageous for Ferracci to run the older chassis during 1994, as this was very well developed and the chassis setup from 1993 could still be utilized. For 1994, the weight for twins was increased to 336 pounds (152 kilograms), but there was considerable controversy over the eligibility of Ferracci's 955. However, Ferracci had the factory develop a special 955 kit that included new cylinders, crankshaft, con-rods, and pistons. After three straight Ducati victories, the weight for twins was increased immediately to that of the fours (358 pounds or 162 kilograms). This certainly evened the odds,

and Corser eventually won the championship by a solitary point.

The 851/888 chassis was the product of continual evolution, and by 1993 was undoubtedly showing difficulty in coping with the demands placed by nearly 150 horsepower in a racing machine. For the first time in three years, a Ducati rider failed to win the World Superbike Championship, and there had really been little development on the chassis since 1986. During that time not only power, but tire technology had improved. As a racing design, the 888 chassis was too long, and with the engine only supported in two locations, the structure was exhibiting deficiencies. Not only was frame rigidity called into question, but the engine was positioned too far rearward, and the entire structure was excessively bulky. Although the final 888s were nicely developed motorcycles, providing excellent power and handling, they were at their peak of development with nowhere left for them to go. Even more power would have stretched the chassis further, as the design was already testing the limit of structural rigidity and weight distribution. Despite Terblanche's excellent facelift, the styling had evolved more by accident than design and was beginning to look dated. Like so many earlier Ducatis, the success of the 888 was purely down to that of evolutionary development, and it was undoubtedly a successful formula. This formula would also work for the next series of Desmoquattro, the 916.

Taking Polen's place in the Fast by Ferracci Team for 1994 was Australian rider Troy Corser. Corser also won the AMA Superbike Championship, but by the narrowest of margins, on the 955-cc Ferracci machine. *Australian Motorcycle News*

Chapter Three

Supermono

Even if the Supermono is currently an anomaly in the world of Desmoquattro Superbikes, when it was conceived, it promised to form the foundation of a new family of single-cylinder motorcycles. The Supermono was always championed by Massimo Bordi, who envisaged it as the perfect single-cylinder motorcycle for both the racetrack and street.

Development got under way during 1990, with Bordi electing to adapt the current 90-degree V-twin so that vibration, the traditional bugbear of big singles, could be eliminated. Bordi's original idea called for a V-twin with a dummy piston, but due to internal friction and crankcase pressure, the 487-cc (95.6x68-mm) engine produced a disappointing 53 horsepower on its first dyno run in the winter of 1990. Even an increase to 57 horsepower was deemed insufficient, so Bordi incorporated a unique counterbalancing system with the second con-rod attached to a lever pivoting on a pin fixed in the crankcase. Titled the *doppia bielletta* (double con-rod), this was the first time it had been used on a gas engine, although it had been used on diesel engines in the past. Bordi had considerable experience with small direct injection diesels, because he was involved with VM diesel development at Ducati from 1978 until he started working on motorcycle engines in 1982. Not only was the revised

Supermono engine more compact, but the twin's perfect primary balance was preserved without the burden of friction. Immediately the power went up to 62.5 horsepower at 10,500 rpm. The next stage saw a 502-cc version (95.6x70 mm) that produced 70 horsepower before the development team led by Gianluigi Mengoli and Claudio Domenicali created a larger cylinder with a wider stud pattern to allow for a "closed deck" Nikasil 100-mm cylinder and a British Omega 11.8:1 piston. This 549-cc example, producing 75 horsepower at 10,000 rpm, was the version that went into limited production during 1993.

Many of the features of the Supermono were inherited from the 888 Racing. Along with liquid cooling, and the double overhead camshaft, four-valve desmodromic cylinder head, it used an identical Weber I.A.W. Alfa/N fuel injection system, with twin injectors and a 435 (P8) CPU. The throttle body diameter was 50 mm, tapering to 47 mm at the butterfly; the valve sizes were 37 and 31 mm, and the camshafts had the same profile as the 926-cc 1994 888 Racing. The camshafts, though, were 10 mm shorter, with the exhaust having a slot machined to provide a takeoff for the water pump impeller. There were some important departures in the design, notably the use of much stronger 49-mm plain main bearings, and a dry 180-watt alternator on the left with the water pump driven off the

The 1992 prototype Supermono looked similar to an 888 Corsa and quite different from the eventual Terblanche version. *Australian Motorcycle News*

Essentially a twin without
the vertical cylinder, the
Supermono engine
provided an exceptionally
low center of gravity. The
hump for the *doppia
bielletta* lever is clearly
evident. *Ian Falloon*

exhaust camshaft. Thus, many engine
components were specific to the Supermono,
including the crankcases, cylinders,
crankshaft, and gearbox with different ratios.
As with the 888 Racing, the two con-rods
were titanium Pankl, with a length of 124
mm, a 21-mm wristpin, and a 42-mm big-end.
Because of the plain main bearings, oil pump
flow was increased up to 3.3 liters per
minute every 1,000 rpm, from 2.6 liters per
minute every 1,000 rpm on the twin. The 50-
mm exhaust exited on the right, into either a
Termignoni single or dual outlet muffler.

Housing this remarkable engine was a
tubular steel frame, designed by Domenicali
and Franco Bilancione and built by Cagiva
Telai in Varese, with an aluminum Verlicchi-
made swingarm. Rather than the usual
25CrMo4 chrome molybdenum steel tubing,
the frame was built of a new material, ALS
500. With 22-mm-diameter tubing, with a
1.5-mm wall thickness, this provided the
same stiffness to weight at a lower cost,
and was TIG-welded and individually crafted.
Domenicali studied 14 different chassis
designs on the CAD system before settling
on the final 6-kilogram design. He measured

both the Yamaha and Aprilia 250-cc Grand
Prix machines to achieve dimensions exactly
between the two. The rear suspension was by
cantilever, but with a nine percent rising rate
due to the mounting angle. Only the highest
quality suspension components were used.
The 42-mm Öhlins upside-down fork with
magnesium triple clamps was similar to the
fork used on the 888 Corsa. The Öhlins
DU2041 shock absorber was adjustable for
ride height via an eccentric.

A steering head angle of 23 degrees,
giving 92 mm (3.62 inches) of trail, and a
compact 1,360-mm (53.5-inch) wheelbase
assured responsive handling. This was 20
mm less than Bordi originally anticipated,
but even more significant was the weight
distribution that placed 54.5 percent on
the front wheel. Marchesini three-spoke
magnesium wheels in sizes of 3.50x17
and 5.00x17 inches were fitted, along with
Brembo 280-mm fully floating iron front discs,
and racing P4.30–34-mm calipers. At the rear
was a 190-mm Brembo disc and P32A caliper
with a torque-arm attached to a carbon-fiber
bracket. In order to keep the weight down to
122 kilograms, every body part was made of

carbon-fiber. There was no rear subframe, the carbon-fiber seat fulfilling this function.

During mid-1992 at Misano, Davide Tardozzi tested a prototype of the Supermono, which was intended for Sounds of Singles racing. This had bodywork similar to the 1992 SP4, but when the Supermono was finally displayed at the Cologne Show in September, it had stunning bodywork by Pierre Terblanche. Only receiving a bare chassis in July, Terblanche worked at Cagiva Morrazone in Varese, creating the bodywork in two months. "The inspiration for the design came from Kork Ballington's wonderful Kawasaki KR 250 and 350-cc Grand Prix machines of the late 1970s, as well as Ducati's own magnificent 750 TT1," says Terblanche. "The tailpiece owes much to the Honda NR 750 while the carbon-fiber seat support came from the Aprilia 250. We made three clay models, then one fiberglass model, and Cagiva Telai modified the frame to allow for the airbox. The only aspect I wasn't particularly pleased with was the exhaust. I wanted this to exit on the left and not the right." When it finally went into production during 1993, the Supermono was a Sounds of Singles racer only, with an individually numbered plaque, and constructed by the racing department.

Only 30 were manufactured in 1993, plus a further 10 in 1994.

Mauro Lucchiari campaigned a factory racing version during 1993 (with a heavily braced swingarm and larger 300-mm front discs), and one was taken to the Isle of Man, where Robert Holden finished second in the 1994 Single Cylinder TT. He came back in 1995 to win easily, setting a fastest lap of 111.66 miles per hour in the process. However, even when it was released, the Supermono was giving away up to 50 percent in capacity to some of the specialized single-cylinder competition and was relying on finesse and balance to achieve success. This led to a larger version for 1995, with a 102-mm piston yielding 572 cc. There also was a revised EPROM and silencer, and slightly different suspension, with 42-mm Öhlins FG 9311 front forks with magnesium triple clamps, and a 10-mm longer DU 2042 rear unit. These examples carried a plaque with a new number sequence, and 25 were constructed. Yet, even this increase in capacity wasn't enough to ensure racetrack dominance, and most of these Supermonos ended in collections rather than on the track. In the European SuperMono Cup, a support event to World Superbike, the Ducati Supermono only won once, at Donington in

One of Pierre Terblanche's most spectacular designs, the Supermono looked like no other motorcycle when it was first displayed in 1992. This is one of the 30 1993 production examples. *Rolf im Brahm*

If ever a motorcycle was a piece of sculpture, it was the Supermono. From every angle it was beautiful, and all the components were of the highest quality.
Ian Falloon

1998 in the hands of Callum Ramsay on the Sigma machine. However, British racing journalist, and one of the most enthusiastic exponents of the Supermono's virtues, Alan Cathcart, came close to winning the series in 1996 on a Vee Two-prepared machine. At Daytona too, Ducati World Superbike Öhlins technician Jon Cornwell won the AHRMA Supermono race in 1998, again on the Sigma 1995 specification machine.

Probably the most important function of the Supermono was its use as a test bed for the World Superbike racers. In 1991, 95.6-mm pistons were tried on the racers, and during 1993, much was learned about piston speeds with a longer stroke and a 100-mm piston on Lucchiari's racer through increasing the revs to 11,500 rpm. Work with the pressurized airbox led to an improved airbox design on the 916 over that of the 888. Thereafter followed a period during which the imminent release of a production Supermono was announced annually. This seemed most likely in 1998, when a Supermono engine was installed in a 900 Supersport frame. Only one was constructed but there were plans to increase the capacity to 600 cc and revert to ball main bearings. Although the Supermono engine had been designed for the inclusion of an electric start, there was no provision to mount a sidestand, and this would have required retooling for series production. Another problem was that the displacement of the Supermono engine couldn't be increased much beyond 600 cc without a major redesign. The development and tooling costs for a 600-cc Supermono seemed to rule it out, and with the departure of its main protagonist, Massimo Bordi, series production appeared unlikely by 2001. However, in a recent discussion with Pierre Terblanche, the author ascertained that all isn't lost for those proponents of the Supermono. "I would still like to see the production of a 90-horsepower, 365-pound (165-kilogram) supercharged Supermono single," says Terblanche. Supercharging would negate the need to create an engine much larger than 600 cc, and when placed in a lightweight chassis, a street version of Supermono could be the ultimate sporting street motorcycle. As Terblanche went on to say, "A supercharged Supermono with that sort of power to weight ratio would make current open class Superbikes look the fat overweight pigs that they are." If Terblanche gets his way, after more than a decade the street Supermono may well eventuate, and it will surely be worth the wait.

Not only beautiful, the Supermono was also spectacularly effective as a racing machine. This is the late Robert Holden, who rode the Supermono to victory in the Isle of Man Singles TT of 1995. *Ian Falloon*

Chapter Four

916 1994–1998

Even though the 888 was proving formidable in World Superbike, the Castiglionis knew this design couldn't last forever. The Japanese were constantly updating their 750 cc Superbikes and it was inevitable that the inequitable weight regulations between twins and fours would change. Therefore, while Massimo Bordi and his team at Bologna were steadily developing the 888, Massimo Tamburini was at work creating a new Desmoquattro, the 916. The 916 also marked a huge change in direction for the company. Ducatis in the past were characterized by evolution, and they used modified existing components where possible, sometimes providing an unbalanced machine. Now Tamburini started with a clean sheet of paper, and while he was tied to the Desmoquattro engine, he would design the entire motorcycle as an entity. Such was his genius that the resulting 916 would not only be one of the finest Ducatis ever built, but one of the finest motorcycles of all time.

Assisted by Massimo Parenti and four engineers, Tamburini embarked on this project (code named 2887) during 1987 at Rimini. It wasn't until 1993 that the Cagiva Research Center was established at San Marino. Interruptions along the way saw development lasting six years; design work on the 916 frame alone took two years before the construction of a prototype. As the project grew the team expanded to include 25 designers and engineers (including Pierre Terblanche), while all along there was consultation with Massimo Bordi back in Bologna. While an aluminum delta box-style frame was considered, tradition won out and the new design retained its links with earlier Ducatis with a tubular steel frame. Racing experience with the 851 and 888 dictated a reduced wheelbase, provide close to 50/50 weight distribution and adequate wheel travel. This meant placing the front wheel as close to the engine as possible, requiring the engine to be rotated forward 1 1/2 degrees to help the front tire clear the cylinder head.

A preliminary mockup appeared during 1991, and by January 1992 the frame configuration was complete and the first of four prototypes was built. With a wheelbase of 55 inches (1,410 mm) and 49 percent of weight on the front wheel, the primary goals were met. Built by Cagiva Telai, the diameter of the main tubing (25 CrMo4) was now 28 mm, with the secondary tubing the same as that on the 888 at 22 mm. An additional lower engine support contributed to increased rigidity and provided additional swingarm support. An important component of the structure was the sealed plastic airbox, with the lower part of the 17-liter fuel tank forming the top of the airbox. A carbon-fiber airbox specified for racing and some Sport

When it was released in 1993, the 916 appeared almost revolutionary in execution, though it was still an evolution of the 888. *Two Wheels*

Production versions increased frame rigidity by 20 per cent. Because the early 916 was conceived as a Monoposto, the rear subframe was aluminum.

One of the significant features of the new frame was its exceptionally strong steering head structure, with 80-mm-diameter tubing and special bearings for the 35-mm steering stem. Adjustable caster was incorporated in the design. The standard setting was 24 1/2 degrees, giving 97 mm of trail. For racing this could be altered to 23 1/2 degrees with 91 mm of trail. The alteration in caster was achieved by ellipsoidal bearings in the steering tube, but with the steeper setting the steering lock couldn't function. A nonadjustable Sachs-Boge steering damper, with symmetrical action mounted transversely below the top triple clamp helped provide neutral steering response.

Few chassis components were shared with the 888. A specially constructed 43-mm Showa GD 051 front fork provided 127 mm of

wheel travel. There were 10 settings for rebound damping, 12 for compression damping, and a 15-mm range for spring preload. Another significant feature was the design of the triple clamps, which were machined in pairs, with an extremely deep chill-cast lower triple clamp.

Because Bordi in particular was still interested in endurance racing, he specified a single-sided swingarm. This would enable rapid wheel changes in endurance events but offered no real advantage in Superbike. It did however contribute to the uniqueness of the design and included additional supporting bearings. There were twin roller bearings on the drive side and twin ball bearings on the right. Constructed of chill-cast aluminum, the 475-mm swingarm was 19 mm shorter than that of the 888. A large eccentric hub provided chain adjustment, and the hollow axle was 35 mm in diameter. The pushrod linkage featured Teflon-lined spherical bearings. The rear suspension was a Showa

GD052-007-02, with a stroke of 71 mm, providing 130 mm of wheel travel. Also new for the 916 were three-spoke 17-inch Brembo wheels, with 3.50 and 5.50-inch rim widths. These wheels featured hollow elliptical spokes with a variable cross-section.

The brakes were similar to those on the 888. At the front were the same stainless steel 320x5-mm discs, with Brembo P4. 30–34 Gold Series brake calipers and a PS 16-mm master cylinder with a remote reservoir. There were no adjustable brake and clutch levers, and the combination of rubber brake lines and Fren-do 222 brake pads gave a soft feel. At the rear was a smaller, 220x6-mm, steel disc with a Gold Series P2.105N caliper and PS 11-mm master cylinder.

Because the 916 was essentially a product of the Cagiva Research Center, many components were unique to this design and not shared with the earlier 888 and 851. This even included bolts and banjo fittings with hollowed out heads. Tamburini took great pride in the special headlight support and the twin polyellipsoidal headlights. Specifically styled twin taillights and an exhaust system that was more than a set of exhaust pipes and mufflers completed the unique look. Designed to aid aerodynamics more than ultimate power, this system also provided excellent access to the rear wheel. A pair of 45-mm header pipes ran into a muffled collector before exiting to 45-mm muffler pipes and 110-mm mufflers. To reduce frontal area and improve aerodynamics over the 851/888, the final design was extremely compact, and when viewed from above, the shape was intentionally designed to emulate the curves of a woman. At 438 pounds (198 kilograms), the 916 was also lighter than the 888 Strada.

While Tamburini was working on the chassis, Massimo Bordi was busy at Bologna adapting the 888 engine for the new design. The goal was always to eventually produce a full liter engine, so Bordi lengthened the stroke 2 mm, to 66 mm. Two 11:1 94-mm pistons similar to those from the 888 Sport Production gave 916 cc of displacement, with the possibility of more displacement through wider bores. Steel Pankl H-section con-rods

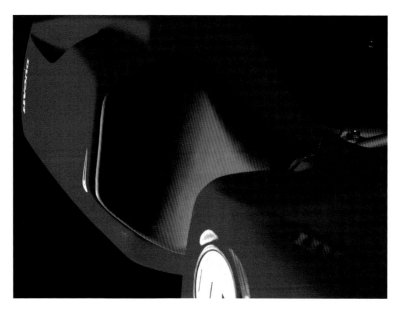

Tamburini's execution of the fuel tank and seat was almost sculptural, the shape intentionally designed to emulate that of a woman. *Two Wheels*

The 916 wasn't only beautiful. As a racing machine with street equipment, it was also an extremely functional sporting motorcycle. *Two Wheels*

with the same 124-mm eye-to-eye length as before weighed 500 grams each. Other con-rod dimensions were shared with the 888, including the 45-mm big-end journal, and 20-mm wristpin. There was an improved left side main bearing, now incorporating an additional ball.

The 33- and 29-mm valves and camshafts were the same as the 888 Strada, and the cylinder head was designed to accept up to 38-mm inlet and 31-mm exhaust valves for racing. Also shared with the 888 Strada was the gearbox, 31/62 2:1 primary drive, and clutch. The Weber Marelli electronic injection and ignition system included a single injector, a 50-mm throttle body, and an I.A.W. 435 (P8) CPU with an 054 EPROM. The CPU was mounted under the tailpiece, above the twin mufflers, and a 350-watt alternator provided the power for the electrical system. Revisions to the cooling system included a curved radiator with an increased surface area. There was also an external oil cooler similar to that of the 888 Sport Production. The claimed power of the 916 Strada was 114 horsepower at 9,000 rpm at the crankshaft.

The 916 was first displayed at the Milan Show at the end of 1993, but production examples were slow to appear. A fire in the paint shop at the factory in Bologna early in 1994 delayed production, and all 2,663 916 Stradas for 1994 were produced at Varese. Because of the extensive development there were few problems for a new model and only limited recalls. Ducati offered four levels of specification of 916s below the factory racers, although the 916 Racing (actually 955 cc) wasn't available until 1995. The 916 SP was the homologation version above the 916 and available through the SP3 of 1996.

In addition to the 916 Strada, there was also a 916 S for 1994. Combining features of the 916 Strada and SP, and primarily intended for the domestic market to satisfy the demand for SPs, 199 were constructed. Except for Termignoni carbon-fiber mufflers, the engine specifications of the 916 S were the same as the Strada, but generally the bodywork was that of the Sport Production. However, in line with the inconsistency of the SP that year, some 916 Ss featured Sport Production seats and carbon-fiber fenders while others didn't.

The 916 Sport Production (1994–1996)

After the success of the 851 and 888 SP, Limited Edition Sport Production series were

For non-U.S. markets in 1995 the 916 was a Biposto. This remained virtually unchanged through 1997. *Australian Motorcycle News*

Following the 888 SP5 was the higher performance 916 Sport Production. This 1994 916 SP has carbon-fiber side panels and rubber brake lines. *Rolf im Brahm*

embedded in Ducati's culture, so it was inevitable that a 916 SP would follow the Strada. Developments for the 916 SP included lighter (12-ounce or 349-gram) titanium H-section Pankl con-rods and twin fuel injectors per cylinder (still with the P8 CPU). The cast-alloy throttle bodies were also 50 mm, but these were from the 888 SP5. The 916 SP also had a new 057 EPROM and, as with the earlier SP series, featured twin roller main bearings. Another distinguishing feature was the cylinder heads, based on those of the 916 Racing without the cast "DESMO 4V DOHC" lettering, providing additional front wheel clearance. The SP crankcases also featured a drilled M8x75-mm crankcase retaining screw beneath the gearbox for extra strength. Because the crankcase and alternator cover gaskets leaked under racing conditions, all 916 SPs used Omnivisc 1002 adhesive instead of gaskets. Another development of the SP over the Strada was a modified lubrication system, also from the Racing 888, featuring forced lubrication to the piston gudgeon pins through a gallery in the con-rod.

As with the earlier SP5, the 916 SP had larger valves (34-mm inlet and 30-mm

exhaust), and more radical camshaft timing. Combined with an 11.2:1 compression ratio, the 916 SP produced 126 horsepower at 10,500 rpm at the crankshaft, although this was later revised to 131 horsepower. Unlike the earlier 888 SP, the 916 SP shared its gearbox with the 916 Strada, but the clutch was from the 888 SP4 and SP5. Some 916 SPs also came with a drilled clutch basket, and the 916 SP had the larger 350-watt alternator of the 916 Strada, rather than the smaller alternator of the earlier 888 SP. There also was a larger-diameter exhaust system, the unmuffled collector box interfacing the 45-mm header pipes with a 50-mm collector box and mufflers. The SP also came with additional Termignoni carbon-fiber mufflers, and a 50-mm racing exhaust system was available.

Although the basic chassis was similar to that of the 916 Strada, the SP featured an Öhlins DU 3420 rear shock absorber and a number of carbon-fiber body parts. These included a front mudguard, chainguard, rear brake line guard, license plate holder, exhaust pipe insulation, front lower fairing panel, and under seat tray, and some had carbon-fiber panels under the fuel tank. Some 1994 916 SPs also came with a carbon-fiber airbox, but

this wasn't universal. As with all previous SPs, the front 320x5-mm disc brakes were fully floating cast-iron, and in an effort to improve braking performance the brake pads changed to Ferodo 450. The weight was down to 424 pounds (192 kilograms). With a top speed of around 168 miles per hour, the 916 SP brilliantly upheld the performance tradition of the earlier Sport Production series. Ducati produced the small number of 1994 916 SPs (310) at the Cagiva factory in Varese. Each SP came with a race stand and red motorcycle cover.

For 1995, the 916 SP was virtually unchanged except for the electrical system. The wiring was altered, and an external power module and 15-amp fuse to protect the ignition and injection system relay was included. While the 916 Biposto received the new 1.6 M CPU, the 916 SP retained the earlier P8 system with a separate rpm sensor and twin injectors per cylinder. Inside the engine the con-rods were now normal Pankl steel, and some 1995 916 SPs featured a drilled clutch basket.

The 1995 916 SP was, visually, almost indistinguishable from the 1994 version, except that the fairing was retained by screws rather than rivets. Although the brakes were unchanged, the 1995 916 SP had stainless steel brake lines and Fren-do brake pads. The frame was reinforced and was now constructed of ALS 450 tubing, and there was an extended carbon-fiber chain cover. Production for 1995

was back at Borgo Panigale, but the production numbers were still very limited, with only 401 manufactured.

For 1996, the 916 SP became the SP3, now with a numbered plaque on the top triple clamp. The engine specifications remained the same as 1995 with steel H-section con-rods but with the new series of crankcases without the earlier kickstart boss. The SP3 crankcases also featured 102-mm (up from 100-mm) cylinder mouths allowing the easy installation of 96-mm pistons, to give 955 cc. There was less carbon-fiber, with an aluminum clutch cover, and plastic exhaust pipe insulating panel. Production of the 916 SP3 was also limited, with only 497 produced.

Also during 1996, a small number (54) of 955-cc SPAs (Sport Production America) were manufactured as homologation specials for AMA Superbike racing. AMA homologation required 50 examples of a production machine sharing its displacement with the racer. Changes from the 916 SP3 included a 96-mm cylinder and piston; lighter crankshaft, with Pankl H-section titanium con-rods; revised final drive gearing; and different lighting. The I.A.W. twin injector system was still a P8, but with a 070 EPROM. Cosmetically, the SPA looked similar to the SP3, with "916" fairing decals, though the engine came with a ZDM955 number series. The SPA was the only production street Ducati to feature a 955-cc engine, and thus, was quite unique.

The 916 Strada

Developments for the 1995 model year saw the 916 Strada became a Biposto (dual seat) in all markets except the United States, where the 916 was still a Monoposto. The Monoposto frame continued with an aluminum rear subframe, and in response to complaints about the rebound damping of the Showa shock absorber, U.S. versions received an Öhlins DU 3420 rear shock absorber. On the Biposto, the rear subframe was steel and all 1995 frames were now of ALS 450 tubing rather than the earlier 25CrMo 4. In addition to the associated footpeg brackets, there was a longer chain cover, and to accommodate the extra weight, the 916 Biposto received a new Showa GD052-007-50 rear shock absorber. Inevitably there was an increase in weight with, the Biposto going up to 451 pounds (204 kilograms).

The most significant development for 1995 was a new electronic ignition and injection system, the 1.6 M. Considerably smaller than the P8, this system also featured a single sensor for phase and rpm from the timing belt jackshaft. One of the intentions was to improve low speed running, but the system relied on an accurate gear drive to the jackshaft. From engine number 002879 there was also a new alternator and regulator. Other changes for 1995 included forged Macchi con-rods instead of the previous H-section Pankl, and screws replaced the rivets for fastening the fairing and screen.

The 916 Senna

Replacing the 916 S for 1995 was the 916 Senna. Following a visit to the Ducati factory in March 1994 by the Brazilian Formula One driver Ayrton Senna, the Castiglionis agreed to produce a special 916 Senna, though the release was delayed due to Senna's death at Imola two months later. Senna was a friend of the Castiglioni brothers and an owner of an 851. The production (301 units) was eventually scheduled for the 1995 model year, with the profits going to the Senna Foundation. The black-and-gray color scheme, with red wheels, set the Senna apart from the regular 916. The engine specification was similar to that of the 916 Strada, but the chassis was shared with the 916 SP. The injection system was the updated 1.6 M type with single injectors, although the Senna engine

The first series of limited production 916 Sennas became available during 1995, combining a 916 Monoposto engine with a Sport Production chassis that featured distinctive colors. *Ian Falloon*

After a hiatus during 1996, a second Senna series appeared for 1997. This was essentially identical to the first version but was painted a lighter gray. *Ian Falloon*

The final Senna was produced for the 1998 model year, now black with the new Vignelli logos. *Ian Falloon*

featured steel Pankl con-rods. The power was 109 horsepower at 9,000 rpm.

Because the Senna came only with a solo seat, there was an aluminum rear subframe. Other quality equipment included an Öhlins DU 3420 rear shock absorber and fully floating cast-iron 320-mm front brake discs. Also shared with the SP were adjustable brake and clutch levers; stainless steel brake lines; and carbon-fiber front fender, clutch cover, chainguard, and exhaust pipe insulating panel. Because of production difficulties, there was no Senna for 1996 but another series, the Senna II, appeared for 1997. Again, 301 were manufactured and these were virtually identical to the earlier version, but were painted a lighter gray. The final series of 300 were produced for the 1998 model year, now painted black and featuring the new Vignelli logos. As before, there was a carbon-fiber front mudguard, chainguard, and license plate bracket. The 1998 version also received a carbon-fiber airbox and exhaust heat shield. As before, there was an Öhlins rear suspension unit and a numbered plaque. Although touted as a

limited production model, the three series of Senna were not quite as exclusive as anticipated. Only providing the performance of a 916 Strada, they also failed to justify a price approaching that of a 916 SP.

1996

With strong demand for the 916, there were few changes for the 1996 model year. The clutch cover incorporated sound absorption material, and there were sound deadening panels in the fairing. There were new crankcases, now without the kickstart boss that was a carryover from the Pantah, and four M8x90-mm screws replaced the previous M8x75- and 85-mm screws. There were a total of 16 retaining screws rather than the previous 14. With production problems continuing through 1996, there were only minimal developments for the 1997 model year, and finally, the 916 Biposto with steel rear subframe, and Showa shock absorber was available in the United States.

The 916 Biposto now received adjustable brake and clutch levers, and from frame number 010082 there were new front brake calipers. From frame number 010233 there were also new 320-mm stainless steel front brake discs, featuring a revised spring loading system. Other improvements during 1997 were the substitution of the Ducati Energia regulator by a Japanese Shindengen, and the fitting of a Bosch fuel pump (from frame number 010532) instead of a Walbro.

The 916 SPS (1997–1998)

Although the 916 Biposto continued with few changes for 1997, there was a major upgrade to the Sport Production series, with the 916 SPS (Sport Production Special). Carrying on from the spectacular 888 SPS of 1992, the 916 SPS was easily the strongest performing production Ducati to that time.

Even though it carried the generic "916" title, central to the 916 SPS was a 996-cc engine to homologate new crankcases for the World Superbike racer. These now had 105-mm crankcase mouth openings, with the cylinder studs spaced 123 mm apart rather than the previous 120 mm. This allowed for thicker (3.5-mm) cylinder liners and required smaller diameter (M6x80-mm) screws at the crankcase mouth. There were 16 crankcase retaining screws.

In addition to the new crankcases, the 916 SPS received a redesigned cylinder head with 36-mm inlet valves and larger intake ports. There also were revised desmodromic camshafts designed to improve midrange power, and the crankshaft was lighter, with

All Sennas had Öhlins rear shock absorbers, and the 1998 version featured more carbon-fiber than earlier examples. *Ian Falloon*

Pankl H-section con-rods. The 11.5:1 98-mm pistons had a low 27.4-mm deck height and the electronic injection system was the earlier twin injector P8, but with a 071 EPROM. The throttle bodies were 50 mm in diameter, and with 50-mm header pipes and Termignoni mufflers, the power was a claimed 134 horsepower at 10,500 rpm at the crankshaft. Other developments included new straight-cut 32/59 primary gears, from the 1996 916 Racing, and the closer ratio 748 gearbox. The basic chassis was identical to that of the 916 SP, and with 916 decals there was little to differentiate the two models. Only the "916 SPS" plaque on the top triple clamp, and the carbon-fiber exhaust shield gave the larger machine away. The 1997 916 SPS was also produced in fewer numbers than later versions, with only 404 manufactured.

After the success of the 1997 916 SPS, the model was offered again for 1998, but with production significantly increased (1,058 produced). In line with all 1998 models there were new Vignelli logos with no tank decals,

and while the general engine specifications were unchanged, there were new titanium con-rods (weighing 13.8 ounces or 395 grams) and revised valve rocker arms. Although the con-rods were no longer Pankl H-section, they were still Pankl, and similar in shape to the regular forged 916 Biposto con-rod.

Because the 916 SPS was still primarily a homologation model for World Superbike racing, there was a new frame, visually identical to before but made of lighter 25CrMo4 steel tubing of thinner section. There was also a carbon-fiber airbox, bringing with it the claimed benefits of increased chassis rigidity. The rest of the chassis was as before, although the Showa front fork was new and the lower sliders had wider front-brake caliper mounts. There was a new gold-series Brembo front brake caliper. Other improvements for 1998 included an Öhlins steering damper, and additional carbon-fiber heat shields and panels. In line with all 1998 model year Ducatis, there was a Shindengen regulator, and no battery charge light incorporated on the dashboard.

Also during 1998, a limited run of Fogarty Replica 916 SPSs were built to homologate a revised frame for World Superbike. Although it only featured a change to the rear bracing tube to increase the airbox volume, this was an extremely successful modification. Despite the frame change, the Fogarty Replica still retained the earlier airbox design. The 202 machines were available only in England, and while they were virtually identical to the regular 916 SPS, there were a few extra touches to justify the premium price. The decals were patterned on the Ducati Performance 996 World Superbike racer of Carl Fogarty, and the wheels were black five-spoke Marchesini rather than the regular gold three-spoke Brembo. The fuel tank, bike cover, and key fob also came with a Fogarty signature. Other features specific to the Fogarty Replica included a titanium exhaust system and a carbon-fiber seat unit with racing Tecnosel seat pad.

Even by the 1998 model year, the 916 remained virtually unchanged and only small details set it apart from earlier examples. The most obvious difference was the Vignelli logos, with no "DUCATI" decal on the fuel tank. Engine developments saw improved timing belts, now Kevlar reinforced and the same as on the racing 916. Every year saw small changes in the lubrication system, and for 1998 there were additional baffles incorporated in the crankcases. In addition to the braided steel front brake lines came similar clutch and rear brake lines. Yellow 916 Bipostos were now available alongside red, and there was a small increase in production with 5,460 916s produced for 1998. The 1998 U.S. 916 was still either a Biposto (with Showa shock absorber), or Monoposto (with an Öhlins shock absorber), and retained the rubber brake lines. Most U.S. 916s were Monoposto. After undergoing evolutionary development for several years, by 1998, the 916's territory as the leading sporting twin was under threat. Production levels were still high (5,460 built in 1998) but for the 1999 model year, the 916 grew to a full 996-cc. However, the 916-cc engine would live on, initially in the ST4 and later in the Monster S4.

Even though it displaced 996 cc, the SPS for 1998 was still titled a 916 SPS. A lighter frame and revised forks and brakes were new this year. *Ian Falloon*

Chapter Five

Superbike Racing 1994–2001

After winning the World Superbike Championship from 1990 through 1992, Ducati had tasted success and wanted this to continue. Even though Ducati won the 1993 constructor's championship, Fogarty's defeat during 1993 left a bitter feeling. So, rather than persevere with the developed 926 racer for another year, Ducati took the plunge with the new, and as yet untried, 916. Because Tamburini designed the 916 as a racer first and a streetbike second, Carl Fogarty managed to provide Ducati with the coveted World Superbike title in 1994. Since then, the process of continual evolution has served Ducati well, and the 916 and its later variants have virtually ruled the World Superbike Championship.

1994

For the 1994 season, Virginio Ferrari replaced Raymond Roche as team manager of the official factory Ducati racing team. Ferrari finished second in the 1979 500-cc World Championship and had a long association with Cagiva and Ducati, winning the Italian Formula One Championship on a factory 750 F1 in 1985. Joining Fogarty on the team again was Giancarlo Falappa, in what was to be his final racing season. Falappa had survived many horrific crashes but a crash while testing at Albacete in June would end his racing career.

This year, the weight of the 750-cc fours was reduced to 353 pounds (160 kilograms), while the twins remained at 320 pounds (145 kilograms). Ducati responded by increasing the displacement of the racer to 955 cc, with 96-mm forged British Omega 11.6:1 pistons. The valve sizes were increased to 37-mm inlet and 31-mm exhaust, and while titanium valves were tried, they were the cause of several engine failures throughout the season. Other engine problems were due to valve rocker failure caused by new camshafts with extremely steep opening and closing ramps. Developed by Luigi Mengoli and Franco Farnè, the new camshafts had long

Despite some early handling problems, Carl Fogarty won the World Superbike Championship on the factory 916 in its 1994 debut season. Ian Falloon

Fogarty won the 1995 World Superbike Championship on the near-perfect factory 955. Ian Falloon

After winning the 1994 AMA Superbike Championship, Troy Corser earned a ride on a factory 955 for 1995. Corser rode for the Austrian Promotor team. *Ian Falloon*

butterfly). With 62.25 psi (or 4.5 bar) fuel pressure and 102 octane AGIP AVGAS, the 955 produced 150 horsepower at 11,000 rpm at the gearbox. The engine was safe to 12,000 rpm and a German KLS electronic gearshift was used, allowing for 1/10th of a second shifting.

Although fitted with a 46-mm Öhlins fork, and an Öhlins rear shock absorber, the 916 racer suffered initial handling problems. To improve traction and place more weight on the front wheel, Tamburini designed a 20-mm-longer magnesium swingarm. The magnesium swingarm weighed 1 kilogram less, helping to push the weight bias forward, and included a 50-mm axle. The wheelbase was increased 0.31 inch (8 mm), to 55.6 inches (1,428 mm), and there was a revised rear suspension lever raising the ride height. To attain the class minimum of 320 pounds (145 kilograms) there were magnesium engine covers, and all the bodywork was in carbon-fiber, with the fairing reinforced by Kevlar. A digital-type instrument panel replaced the analog instrument panel, saving a further 6.63 pounds (3 kilograms). Ducati used carbon brakes for the final time in 1994. The factory 916 racer featured twin Brembo 320-mm or 290-mm carbon discs on the front, shrouded in carbon-fiber covers. At the rear was a 200-mm carbon disc. The wheels were three-spoke—and later five-spoke—Marchesini, a 3.50x17-inch

duration with moderate valve lift, 11-mm inlet and 10.5-mm exhaust. There were titanium Pankl con-rods with 21-mm wristpins. The injection system was a P8 CPU, mounted in the fairing in front of the steering head, with separate EPROM mapping for each cylinder and 50-mm throttle bodies (46-mm at the

The 1996 factory racer undressed. This was still good enough for Corser to win the World Superbike Championship but since it now displaced 996 cc, reliability suffered. *Ian Falloon*

on the front with a 6.00x17-inch on the rear.

Because the racing department could only produce 14 of the 916 Racing machines, which displaced 955 cc, during 1994, only selected riders received them. These were provided to Fabrizio Pirovano riding for Davide Tardozzi, and James Whitham for Moto Cinelli. There were also occasional World Superbike rides for Troy Corser with the Fast by Ferracci 916 Racing. Development of the factory 955 was hampered after Fogarty broke his wrist at Hockenheim in May, but he came back to win the 1994 World Superbike Championship with 10 victories. Falappa and Whitham also won races. Although the championship went down to the final race of the season, the result vindicated the decision to race the new design.

1995

Six official factory 916 racers were available for 1995, and were provided to Virginio Ferrari's ADVF team and the Austrian Promotor team of Alfred Inzinger. Carl Fogarty remained with Ferrari, joined by Mauro Lucchiari, and Troy Corser rode the Promotor entry, managed by Davide Tardozzi. To ensure adequate points for the constructor's championship there were also the satellite entries of Andreas Meklau, Promotor, and Fabrizio Pirovano, Taurus Ducati.

Further development of the 955 over the winter saw it totally dominant at the beginning of the 1995 season. With the initial minimum weight increased to only 325 pounds (147 kilograms) for twins, Fogarty and Lucchiari raced away from the rest of the field in the opening rounds. Engine development concentrated on improving reliability rather than outright power, and there were stronger crankcases, now without the kickstart boss, and new nimonic (a type of material) valves (still 37 and 31 mm). Generally, the engine displaced 955 cc with 11.8:1 96-mm Omega pistons but in the first and final races, Fogarty tried a 996-cc engine with 98-mm pistons. Fogarty was happier with the 955. The larger engine didn't produce more top-end power, but gave around 12 horsepower more at 8,500 rpm, and had a detrimental effect on the handling. A slipper clutch aided the rideability of the 955. With 52-mm exhausts, and running on unleaded fuel as required that year, the power was 154 horsepower at 12,000 rpm at the crankshaft. Fogarty didn't suffer a single mechanical failure all season—his only retirement was due to an electrical fault.

Replacing Carl Fogarty in the ADVF squad for 1996 was John Kocinski. Kocinski started the season well, but by the end of the season he was barely communicating with Virginio Ferrari.
Ian Falloon

Despite improved reliability through newly homologated crankcases, the 1997 factory racer was difficult to ride. *Ian Falloon*

The most successful rider in the history of the World Superbike Championship is Briton Carl Fogarty. Fogarty won four titles for Ducati, and amassed an unmatched 59 race wins, 55 of them on Ducatis. *Ian Falloon*

Ducati's success in the first three rounds saw a revision of the minimum weights, and from Monza onward the twins were required to weigh 343 pounds (155 kilograms), with the 750 fours reduced to 336 pounds (160 kilograms). To increase the weight, a nonfunctioning starter motor was installed, and lead ballast added under the seat. Regulations required steel brake discs, and

Brembo provided twin 320-mm discs for the front and a 220-mm on the rear, along with Brembo P4.32–36 and P2.24 calipers. A 46-mm Öhlins fork was retained, along with an Öhlins shock absorber. The wheels were five-spoke Marchesini, a 3.50x17-inch on the front and a 6.25x17-inch on the rear.

Although Fogarty and the 955 were clearly the superior combination, some of Ducati's advantage was due to the use of electronic telemetry during qualifying, and recruiting Anders Andersson as a full-time Öhlins suspension technician. With an unequaled 20 World Superbike victories in 1955, Fogarty winning 13, the 955 factory racer also provided an optimum balance between power, reliability, and handling that was difficult to replicate. As the demands of competition required more horsepower, and regulations saw increased weight, future versions of the 916 and 996 Racing struggled to match the fine balance of that 1995 model.

During 1995 there also was a modest return to Endurance racing, with two 955 Endurance racers entered in the Bol d'Or in September. Andreas Meklau teamed with Mauro Lucchiari while Stéphane Chambon put the other 955 on pole position. Although the new reinforced crankcases survived 36 hours on the test bench and promised increased reliability, both of the works machines retired.

1996

With Carl Fogarty vacating the Ducati camp for Honda, Virginio Ferrari signed former 250-cc World Champion John Kocinski as his replacement. Joining Kocinski was the young British rider Neil Hodgson, and this year the ADVF team drew on outside sponsorship from Kremlyovskaya Vodka. Again Ducati supported Inzinger's Promotor team, with Corser receiving full factory machinery. American Mike Hale joined Corser, though his equipment wasn't to the same specification. In addition to the six official machines, Pietro di Gianesin's Gattolone team also received factory support. Gianesin did his own engine preparation and his rider, Pier Francesco Chili, won two races.

This year saw the exclusive use of the 996-cc engine, but there were many engine failures. The 12:1 three-ring Omega 98-mm pistons required smaller diameter cylinder studs (6 mm) but the restricted stud spacing allowed for only a 3-mm-thick liner. Most

engine failures were the result of the cylinder liner breaking where it entered the crankcase, although there were also oil pressure problems caused by wheelies. The 37- and 31-mm valves were now a composite design (titanium with steel at the top of the stem to reduce wear), and there were new 32/59 (1.84:1) primary gears. There were also thicker crankcase castings, and a larger airbox (with larger ducts), the space for this was created by moving the radiator header tank forward. This year the engine side covers were aluminum rather than magnesium. Further development included 5-mm throttle bodies, (48-mm at the butterfly), 54-mm-diameter exhausts, and larger water and oil radiators. The fuel pressure was increased to 72.5 psi (5 bar) and the power was 157 horsepower at 11,800 rpm at the gearbox.

World Superbike regulations now required the weight of the twins to be 358 pounds (162 kilograms), the same as the 750-cc fours, so the emphasis was placed on increasing the front end bias. With the increase in weight, the brakes were stretched to the limit. A wider 46-mm Öhlins fork spread the discs 28-mm farther apart for improved cooling. The front Brembo calipers were P4.34–36-mm and there was a new Öhlins rear suspension unit. The five-spoke magnesium Marchesini wheels now measured 3.50x17-inch front and 6.00x17-inch rear. Adding 4.42 pounds (2 kilograms) to the

overall weight was the PI System 3 Plus data acquisition system, now permanently installed.

Preseason testing indicated Kocinski was well suited to the Ducati, and this was further emphasized by his emphatic double victory at the opening World Superbike round at Misano. However, during the season the breakdown in communication between Kocinski and Ferrari destroyed the team's morale and performance, allowing Corser to take the title with seven race wins. The 916 Racing was also extremely successful in European Superbike Championships. Paolo Casoli won the Italian Superbike Championship, Christer Lindholm the German Pro Superbike Championship, and Andreas Meklau the Austrian Superbike Championship.

The 916 Racing (1994–1998)

For 1995, the catalog factory racer was the 916 Racing, closely patterned on Fogarty's 1994 factory bike. The 916 Racing displaced 955 cc, had identical camshaft timing and valve sizes, and featured the closer ratio gearbox from the 1994 racer. First gear was now 32/16; second 29/18; third 27/20; fourth 25/21; fifth 24/22; sixth; 23/23. As with the 1994 888/926 Racing, the I.A.W. injection system featured twin injectors and a 435 (P8) CPU. The compression ratio was 12:1 and the 916 Racing produced 155 horsepower at 11,500 rpm. In the World Superbike Championship Pier Francesco Chili rode Pietro di Gianesin's Team Gattolone machine and won a World Superbike race at Monza.

The chassis specification also reflected developments that had proven successful during 1994. There was a 0.39 inch (10 mm) longer swingarm giving a wheelbase of 49.7 inches or 1,420 mm, and a larger carbon-fiber fuel tank (22 liters). The front suspension was by Öhlins: 46-mm FG 9650 fork, with an Öhlins DU 5360 rear shock absorber. Brembo supplied full racing specification brakes, twin 320-mm cast-iron discs with P4.32–36-mm calipers, and a 19-mm master cylinder. At the rear was a 200-mm disc with a P2.24-mm master cylinder and 11-mm master cylinder. The wheels were five-spoke Marchesini, a 3.50x17-inch on the front and 6.00x17-inch on the rear. While the street 916 (and 916 SP) now used a frame constructed of ALS 450, the 916 Racing continued with the 25CrMo4 frame of the 1994 916. Weight was 340 pounds (154 kilograms). Sixty 916 Racing machines were constructed for 1995.

There was a further batch of 31 955 Racing machines built for 1996. Apart from the lack of air vents in the rear tail section, these were visually identical to the 1995 916 Racing, but there were a large number of hidden changes. Engine developments included new crankcases, aluminum sidecovers, new pistons, and new con-rod bearings. There were also new camshafts with the inlet patterned on those of the 1995 factory racers. The exhaust system was enlarged to 52 mm, with new mufflers, a clutch with a back torque limiter, a steel gearshift selector drum, new timing belts, and an oil pump with an enclosed relief valve. With a slightly lower, 11.8:1 compression ratio, the power was 153 horsepower at 11,000 rpm. Chassis developments saw a new 46-mm Öhlins fork (now with a top-out spring), thicker front brake discs (6 mm), and an aluminum casing and fast preload adjuster for the Öhlins DU 5360 rear shock absorber. The fuel capacity was now 23 liters, and the weight 160 kilograms.

Ducati produced just 20 996 Racing machines for 1997. These reflected the developments on the factory machines during 1996. The crankcases were the newly homologated 916 SPS type; the engine displaced 996 cc, with 98-mm 12:1 pistons. The power was 155 horsepower at 11,000 rpm. There was a new exhaust camshaft, new valve rocker arms, and in line with the 1996 factory bikes, a 32/59-tooth primary drive. The fuel pressure was increased to 72.5 psi (5 bar) and there was a larger capacity airbox, a larger oil radiator, and 54-mm exhaust headers. Chassis developments included the adjustable offset triple clamps of the 1996 factory racer, a larger air intake in the front

From 1993 until moving to the AMA Superbike Championship series in 2001, Andreas Meklau was one of Ducati's racing stalwarts in the World Superbike Championship. Along the way he managed to win Austrian Championships on 916 Racing machines. Here he is during 1995. *Ian Falloon*

fairing, and a new handlebar and rear wheel hub assembly.

There were 24 916 Racing machines produced for 1998, and the general specification continued to be that of the factory machines in the previous year. Although most of the 1997 engine specifications were retained, there was a new crankshaft and con-rod assembly, along with an improved primary drive and spline coupling. Small developments to aid reliability saw different crankshaft shimming, a new crankshaft inlet oil seal, and bigger rimmed timing belt rollers. The larger capacity water radiator was thicker, with three extra rows. A new gearshift drum smoothed gearshifts, and the injection system now included 60-mm throttle bodies with new inlet manifolds, still with the twin injector P8. The valve sizes remained at 37 and 31 mm, and the claimed power was 151 horsepower at 11,000 rpm.

Also new for 1998 was a revised chassis, the TIG-welded 25CrMo4 frame using 1.5-mm tubing, a lighter rear subframe, and a longer magnesium swingarm. This increased the wheelbase to 55.8 inches (1,430 mm), also improving the weight distribution. The 46-mm Öhlins fork was from the 1997 factory

bike, and the Öhlins rear shock absorber featured hydraulic adjustment for the spring preload. Ducati provided 290-mm front brake discs in addition to the standard 320-mm front discs. There was a larger, and reshaped, 24-liter fuel tank, and the weight was 340 pounds (154 kilograms), allowing fine tuning of the weight distribution through ballast.

1997

The American-based Texas Pacific Group bought out Ducati toward the end of 1996. One of the first results of that buyout was an expansion of the World Superbike racing program for 1997. Following a problem with the Kremlyovskaya sponsorship, there was no outside sponsor. Virginio Ferrari's team received full works support from the factory. Carl Fogarty returned to the Ferrari team, while Neil Hodgson retained his ride for a second year. Also receiving factory support was Andrea Merloni's Gattolone Team, with rider Pier Francesco Chili. This year, eight factory machines were produced.

The main development for 1997 was the homologation of new crankcases via the 916 SPS, with wider cylinder stud spacing for thicker cylinder liners with the 98-mm

Fogarty unexpectedly won his third World Superbike Championship in 1998, after Corser crashed in the warm-up to the final race. Fogarty rode for Davide Tardozzi's Ducati Performance team that year. *Ian Falloon*

pistons. These crankcases were heavier so there were fewer requirements for ballast. During 1997 a bolt-on sump extension was successfully tried to alleviate the oil pressure drop under acceleration and braking. The new cylinder heads had larger inlet ports, a revised combustion chamber, and there was a new gearbox, with a lower first (32/16) and higher second (33/21) gear. There was a new exhaust system, larger capacity oil and water radiators, and an increase in the throttle body diameter to 60 mm. Despite regulations requiring a reduction in exhaust levels to 102 db/A (from 105 db/A), the power was around 168 horsepower at 11,300 rpm at the gearbox.

There was a new frame, 3.3 pounds (1.5 kilograms) heavier than before, and in an effort to provide more weight on the front wheel, the cast-magnesium swingarm was 4.4 pounds (2 kilograms) lighter. The 46-mm Öhlins forks had magnesium sliders and a new top-out spring, with the travel increased 5 mm to 125 mm. The 320-mm stainless steel brake discs were 1 mm thicker and spaced more widely apart for additional

Almost as dominant as in 1995, Fogarty easily won the 1999 World Superbike Championship on the Ducati Performance 996.
Ian Falloon

cooling, and Brembo supplied new front brake calipers with larger pistons. The only other change to the chassis specification was a reduction in rear wheel rim width, to 5.75x17-inch, and a slight reshaping of the carbon-fiber-and-Kevlar fuel tank with an increase in capacity to 24 liters.

While the engine developments aided reliability, 1997 was the first year since 1990 that Ducati failed to win the World Superbike constructor's championship. The riders struggled to come to terms with the power delivery and steering response. The 60-mm throttle bodies and lighter crankshaft provided an aggressive power delivery that upset the handling, and there was a problem with the weight distribution that could no longer be easily rectified. A number of new features were tried, including an even longer swingarm, smaller (290-mm) front brake discs to quicken the steering response, and higher profile Michelin rear tires.

Although Fogarty remained unhappy with the performance of the 996, openly stating that he preferred his 1995 955, he still managed second place in the World

Superbike Championship with six victories. Chili also complained about the power delivery and for Brands Hatch was provided with a new EPROM. The improvement enabled him to win the first race, and may have even won the second if Fogarty hadn't taken him down. Chili won three races, and it was a disappointing year for the factory in World Superbike. However, Serafino Foti won the Italian Superbike Championship, and Andreas Meklau again took out the Austrian Superbike Championship.

1998

A further expansion of the racing program for the 1998 World Superbike Championship saw 18 factory 996 racers built, again with three riders supported in two official teams. Troy Corser returned to the Ferrari Team alongside Chili, and Fogarty moved to the new Team Ducati Performance, managed by Davide Tardozzi.

Considerable development was undertaken to improve the 996, and there was a new electronic injection system, a Magnetti Marelli MF3-S system derived from Ferrari Formula One racing. A major advantage of the new system was the ability to download data through a laptop computer connected to the onboard computer via a

Marelli DAS3 data acquisition system. Retaining the 60-mm throttle bodies, the MF3-S system also incorporated a third injector located outboard from each velocity-stack and inside the sealed airbox. Only operating at 70 percent to full throttle when the primary injectors were shut off, because these third injectors were positioned further from the inlet valve, they helped cooler, denser air enter the combustion chamber. Redesigned air intakes and airbox and a new Termignoni exhaust system with reverse cones incorporated in the mufflers complemented the new injection system. The power was around 163 horsepower at 12,000 rpm at the rear wheel. Other engine improvements included a crankcase sump extension with a lower oil pickup, first tried during 1997.

The factory experimented with new swingarms, as well as revising fork triple clamps and chassis settings in an attempt to improve handling. The engine was located slightly more forward in a 25CrMo4 frame that was not as stiff as earlier versions so as not to exaggerate suspension problems. For the first time. Öhlins supplied Grand Prix quality suspension, the 46-mm forks having magnesium sliders and the triple clamps providing variable offset. At the rear, a new Öhlins TT44 rear suspension unit was tried,

Smaller diameter front forks and Brembo radial front brake calipers were new for 1999. *Ian Falloon*

and used occasionally. The TT44 featured "double tube" technology from Formula One and Indy car racing, and used separate twin internal oil tubes for compression and rebound damping. The Brembo front brakes were either 320-mm or 290-mm steel discs, with a choice of two- or four-pad front brake calipers. The quest for improved steering and traction led to experimentation with different wheel sizes, including both 16- and 17-inch front Marchesinis, and either 16.5-inch or 17-inch rear wheels. The change in weight distribution saw 53/54 percent on the front wheel, with 46/47 percent on the rear wheel, and the 1998 racer was significantly improved over the 1997 version.

Early in the season, the 996 lacked power, but this improved following the South African round at Kyalami in early July. Here a new frame—homologated through the 916 SPS Fogarty Replica—allowed the rear

bracing tube to be moved back and downward, also locating the engine slightly lower. Altering one of the top transverse frame tubes under the fuel tank provided room for a larger airbox, with the air intake, throttle bodies, and shorter intakes inside the airbox itself. New cylinder heads positioned the exhaust camshafts closer to the center of the engine to provide more front wheel clearance; this also allowed the incorporation of a different valve angle to improve fuel delivery. Combined with new camshafts, these developments provided a dramatic improvement. The torque curve became flatter, there was even more top-end power (reputedly seven to eight horsepower), and the handling improved. This small modification was the most effective development to the 916 since its inception. At the first race, at Kyalami, 996s filled the top three places. Fogarty narrowly won his

Fogarty in action on the Team Ducati Infostrada machine for the last time, at Phillip Island in 2000. A crash here ended his racing career. *Ian Falloon*

third World Superbike title after Corser crashed in the warm-up at Sugo. The 996 also won the Italian and German Superbike Championships, Paolo Blora winning in Italy, and Andreas Meklau in Germany.

The 996 RS

As increased emphasis was now placed on winning national Superbike championships, a higher specification 996 Racing Special was offered to selected teams for 1999. This incorporated the MF3-S electronic injection system (with 60-mm throttle bodies and three injectors), and the revised frame with larger airbox of the post-Kyalami 1998 factory racers. The 996 RS had larger titanium valves (39-mm inlet and 32-mm exhaust), factory ported cylinder heads, shorter inlet tracts, and a higher lift inlet camshaft (13-mm). There was a sump extension in the crankcase and the lubrication system was upgraded to pump 3.3 liters of oil per minute. There were shorter Termignoni mufflers and the 996 RS produced around seven to eight more peak horsepower than the 996 Racing of 1998. There also were upgraded specification four-

pad Brembo brakes, a 46-mm Öhlins FG 8750S fork, and a DV 7290 rear shock absorber. Eleven 996 RSs were produced for 1999, and they were very successful with Troy Bayliss winning the British Superbike Championship and Steve Martin the Australian Superbike Championship. Also for 1999 was a slightly lower specification 996 Racing, though only six were produced. The main difference between the 996 Racing Special and 996 Racing was in the injection system, the 996 Racing retained the twin injector I.A.W. P8 CPU, with a revised 442 (instead of 435) unit.

A further batch of 10 996 Racing Specials were produced for 2000 for selected teams in the World Superbike and various national championships. The specification included the revised single-injector MF3-S Marelli injection system and a 57-mm stainless steel exhaust system. These 162-horsepower 996 RS 2000s were surprisingly close in performance to the official Team Ducati Infostrada machines, as evidenced by Neil Hodgson's performances on the GSE entry in the 2000 World Superbike Championship.

In the hands of British rider Neil Hodgson, the 996 RS has proved an equal to the factory machinery. Hodgson won two rounds of the World Superbike Championship in 2000 and was a frontrunner throughout 2001. *Ian Falloon*

While the official factory racers were using the new 998-cc Testastretta engine for 2001, the customer 996 RS retained the earlier 996-cc engine. With the shorter intake system of the 2000 factory racers, the power was increased to 168 horsepower at 12,000 rpm. The forks were now 42-mm Öhlins, with radial caliper Brembo front brakes. As with all Superbikes this year, 16.5-inch wheels were fitted front and rear. Again Hodgson proved surprisingly competitive against the new-generation factory machines.

1999

There was a reorganization of the racing program for 1999, and the establishment of a new company, Ducati Corse, headed by Claudio Domenicali. Ducati Motor's complete ownership of Ducati Corse provided more control over the racing program. With only one World Superbike team, Team Ducati Performance, managed by Tardozzi, the factional problems that occurred between Virginio Ferrari, Pier Francesco Chili, and Carl Fogarty during 1998 would hopefully be eliminated. Because there also was more emphasis on winning the AMA Superbike Championship, only Fogarty and Corser

represented the factory in the World Superbike Championship. There were still a number of assisted customer teams on 996 RSs filling out the grid.

Thicker cylinder head castings provided increased rigidity, along with improved porting and reangled valves. A new airbox and intake tracts were used, along with the same triple injector MF3-S injection system with differential mapping between the cylinders. Also available was a choice of two different gearboxes, the Evolution gearbox with taller first and second gears, but gearbox experimentation still required complete engine substitution. During the season, the stainless steel exhaust system was increased to 57 mm. With 168 horsepower at 11,500 rpm, the biggest improvement for 1999 was less power dropoff throughout the range, and a noticeable increase in engine reliability.

Fogarty still wanted to replicate the balance of the 1995 955 racer. The bike featured a smaller diameter (42-mm) Öhlins front fork, in an attempt to improve front tire feel. While not as stiff, they reduced unsprung weight and provided mounts for the new generation of Brembo radial four-piston brake calipers. These improved braking action,

Troy Bayliss came along at the right time, capably filling Fogarty's shoes and providing the new Testastretta with the 2001 World Superbike Championship. *Ian Falloon*

because the calipers were more rigidly located on the fork slider. The smaller 290-mm discs also contributed to improved steering response. There was also a new Öhlins TT44 shock absorber with all new hydraulics, and a revised rear suspension linkage. To reduce rear wheel chatter, this featured a 2:1 constant rate. A slimmer, lower fuel tank that extended more into the airbox was also homologated.

Right from the outset, the combination of Fogarty and the 996 dominated the 1999 World Superbike Championship. At last the fine balance of that 1995 version was replicated, and Fogarty won 11 races during the season. Corser's three race wins and victory at Laguna Seca by Anthony Gobert and Ben Bostrom further emphasized the superiority of the 996 this year. Undoubtedly, much of this was due to the continual evolution of the design. Paolo Casoli was the official Ducati Corse testing and development rider, and on the 996 Factory Evolution racer he won every round of the Italian Superbike Championship. The 996 served as a test bed for World Superbike, and continual improvements filtered through from the Italian series. The single-injector fuel injection

system, however, was held over for 2000 with the throttle butterfly even closer to the valves.

AMA Superbike Racing

The prized championship that has evaded Ducati since 1994 is the AMA Superbike Championship. During 1995, with Corser moving to World Superbike, Eraldo Ferracci recruited former Grand Prix World Champion Freddie Spencer and Mike Smith to ride the 916. Although Spencer won at Laguna Seca in the rain, his overall performance was disappointing, leading to the signing of Larry Pegram and Shawn Higbee for 1996. Poor results then prompted Ducati to enter 1992 125-cc World Champion Alessandro Gramigni in four races. Gramigni immediately impressed—winning at Elkhart Lake and Brainerd—but it wasn't enough to win the championship.

After an impressive 1996 AMA debut season, Ferracci signed Australian Matthew Mladin for 1997. Gerald Rothman Jr. joined Mladin on the team, but this year factory support was also provided to the Vance & Hines Ducati team. Vance & Hines hired former champion Thomas Stevens, also recruiting German Pro Superbike Champion

There were two factory World Superbike teams for 2001, with Ben Bostrom riding for L&M on Dunlop tires. For many events, the tobacco company sponsorship logos were required to be blanked out. *Ian Falloon*

Christer Lindholm for the final race. Again the Ducati line-up looked strong, and while Mladin won four races, inconsistency robbed him of the title. For 1998, Ducati supported two, two-rider teams. Mike Hale and Tom Kipp rode for Ferracci, with Anthony Gobert and Thomas Stevens for Vance & Hines. Gobert won three races with a factory machine, but his off-field antics ruined any chance of his taking the championship.

Gobert was given another chance on the Vance & Hines machine for 1999, now joined by number one AMA plate-holder Ben Bostrom; in the Ferracci team were Matt Wait and Larry Pegram. The 996 Factory machines were similar to the World Superbike racers, but with 54-mm throttle bodies as required by the AMA, 46-mm Öhlins forks, and Dunlop tires. The increase in factory support was immediately evident in the results, but again Gobert let the team down. He won five races but failed to show up for the final event, and Bostrom narrowly lost the championship. As a consolation, Ducati won the manufacturer's title.

Fresh from his success in Britain, Troy Bayliss was signed alongside Steve Rapp in the Vance & Hines team for 2000. With Ferracci losing his factory support, Tim Pritchard's Ohio-based Competition Accessories team leased a 996 RS for Larry Pegram. Bayliss' career in the United States, however, didn't last long, as he was soon called to replace an injured Fogarty in the World Superbike Team. John Kocinski came in as a stand-in, but results were disappointing and Vance & Hines lost its factory support for 2001. This went to Hansen Motorcycles of Manitowoc, Wisconsin, as well as the Competition Accessories Team, though the machines were now 996 RSs instead of factory bikes. The surprise signing for Hansen was that of 1993 World Superbike Champion, and five-time Daytona 200 winner, Scott Russell. Russell received a one-year contract alongside Steve Rapp, but his season ended after a horrific start line accident at Daytona. Later stalwart Austrian Ducati rider Andreas Meklau replaced him, bringing significant sponsorship from the exhaust manufacturer Remus. The Competition Accessories Team retained Larry Pegram, initially also signing John Kocinski and later Aaron Slight, but neither ride eventuated. As it transpired, the 2001 AMA season ended as one of the most disappointing ever for Ducati, and for 2002 there was only one official factory entry, the HMC 998 for Pascal Picotte.

2000

As expected, the official Team Ducati Infostrada retained Carl Fogarty, but surprisingly, Corser's contract wasn't renewed. Signed alongside Fogarty was former AMA Superbike Champion Ben Bostrom. Although it looked as if Carl Fogarty would continue to provide Ducati with World Superbike Championship success, Fogarty's crash at Phillip Island early in the season ended this prospect. Finding a replacement for Fogarty wasn't easy. Test rider Luca Cadalora failed, and it was eventually 31-year-old British Superbike Champion Troy Bayliss who managed to fill Fogarty's shoes. Bostrom experienced considerable difficulty adapting

to the factory machine and its Michelin tires, and after only a few rounds was relegated to the factory-supported NCR team on Corser's 1999 racer. Replacing Bostrom in the Infostrada line-up was Juan Borja, but his results were disappointing.

For the factory machines there were new cylinder heads this year homologated through the 996 Factory Replica 2, with more material around the studs to improve stiffness and solve head gasket sealing problems. There was also more material around the ports, leaving room for future development, but the titanium valve sizes remained at 39-mm inlet and 32-mm exhaust. Computer simulation allowed for a complete reconfiguration of valve timing, compression ratio, porting, throttle body design, and injector position. Thus, there was an even higher compression ratio (over 13:1), and the new desmodromic camshafts provided less overlap.

Another improvement was to the injection system. Tested by Paolo Casoli during 1999 on the 996 Factory Evolution, this retained the Marelli MF3-S CPU and 60-mm throttle bodies, but with a single injector. The single

Matthew Mladin rode for Ferracci during 1997, also failing in his quest for the AMA Superbike title.
Cycle World

Although he had a troubled season during 2000, Ben Bostrom finally came to terms with the factory Ducati during 2001. Winner of the AMA Superbike Championship in 1998, Bostrom looks set to be another American World Superbike Champion. *Ian Falloon*

Generally the chassis for 2000 was the same as 1999, but there were revisions to the internal cartridge of the 42-mm Öhlins fork, and different internal bleeding for the Öhlins shock absorber. The Marchesini wheels were still 3.5x17-inch front and either 6.00x17 or 16.5-inch on the rear. Previously, the factory racers weighed slightly over the 358 pounds (162 kilograms) minimum, but this year the weight was reduced near to the minimum. Preseason testing also saw experimentation with a double-sided swingarm, with high exiting exhausts similar to an 888. However, these experiments proved inconclusive and the single-sided swingarm was retained. This was 15 mm longer than that of the road bike, giving a wheelbase of 55.5 inches or 1,425 mm. There was also an updated Magneti Marelli data acquisition system, with more channels and memory increased to 24 MB, up from 2 MB.

While the 996 factory racer was undeniably improved for 2000, the loss of Fogarty early in the season, combined with Bostrom's difficulties left the Infostrada Team struggling. It wasn't until Monza that Bayliss proved he was capable of running at the front, but at this late stage, winning the championship was virtually impossible. Bayliss went on to win two races, and, fortunately for Ducati, British riders Neil Hodgson and John Reynolds on 996 RSs won three. Hodgson was particularly impressive on the GSE 996 RS.

2001

The next generation Desmoquattro, the Testastretta, was finally released in 2001, after it had been rumored for several years. Although many expected the new engine to appear in a revised chassis, this didn't eventuate, and the Testastretta epitomized Ducati's commitment to an evolutionary approach of development. The chassis was as before, and the engine was also strongly derived from the earlier 996. Following the team difficulties of the 2000 season, and the official retirement of Carl Fogarty following tests at Mugello in September 2000, there was a new team line-up for 2001. Bayliss took Fogarty's position in the Team Ducati Infostrada, joined by the 23-year old Spanish rider Ruben Xaus who moved up from the World Supersport class. Xaus was a protégé of Carl Fogarty and was seen as a future star.

injector was positioned above the throttle valve, and shorter or longer bell mouths could also be used, depending on the power requirements for individual tracks. Also homologated were 50–60-mm shorter intakes, with the throttle bodies closer to the cylinder head. Because of the conical shape of the inlet tract, these acted as if they were larger in diameter and flowed more. There were titanium Termignoni mufflers and, as in previous years, the power increase was around five horsepower. However, not only was the maximum power at a higher 12,000 rpm, with the rev limiter set at 12,500 rpm, but the power curve was improved with more midrange. With 173 horsepower, the evolutionary process had yielded an increase of 15 horsepower over the previous three years.

After improved performances in the later part of the 2000 season, Ben Bostrom was again elevated to the status of a full works rider. For 2001, though, he rode in a separate L&M-sponsored team, on his preferred Dunlop tires, but still under the direction of Tardozzi.

Central to the Ducati Corse World Superbike racing program for 2001 was the 998-cc Testastretta. Only the three official riders received the new engine for the 2001 season. The Testastretta engine featured a larger (100-mm) bore and shorter (63.5-mm) stroke. The cylinder heads were new, with a narrower included valve angle, described in more detail in Chapter 9. Inherited from the earlier 996 were the same 60-mm throttle body and MF3S Magneti Marelli electronic injection and ignition module with a single Marelli IWF1 injector per cylinder. Incorporated in the Testastretta design too was the crankcase sump extension that had earlier only featured on the racing engines. Although

a Marelli semiautomatic gearbox was tested prior to the season, this wasn't raced, and the gearbox was identical to the 2000 model 996. The cooling system was extensively revised, and in its earliest development phase the 998 produced 174 horsepower at 12,000 rpm, with a maximum of 12,500 rpm.

While the Verlicchi frame was as before, as was the rear Öhlins suspension unit, the Öhlins 42-mm front fork featured a sealed hydraulic cartridge, and a low friction spring, as the fork was now pressurized. Brembo continued to develop the braking system, and vented steel discs also were tested. These were 290 to 305 mm on the front and 218 mm on the rear, the advantage coming through reduced operating temperatures. The wheel sizes for 2001 were standardized to 16.5-inch front and rear, with the rear rim width either 6.00 or 6.25 inch. Homologated through the production 996 R was also a new fairing, without the upper side air scoops.

Bostrom demonstrating the style that took him to five consecutive World Superbike race victories during 2001. *Ian Falloon*

Consistent riding during 2001 saw Bayliss become the fifth Ducati rider to win the World Superbike Championship. *Ian Falloon*

races in succession to equal Fogarty's previous record. Xaus too finally rewarded Ducati's faith in him with his first World Superbike victory at Oschersleben, also giving Ducati its 10th manufacturer's title. But it was Bayliss who took out the title with double wins at Assen, becoming Ducati's fifth World Superbike Champion. The result was also a vindication of the brilliance of Ducati's engineers and the excellence of the Testastretta design. At the final round at Imola, Bayliss raced with a silver paint scheme replicating the Imola 200 Formula 750 racers of nearly 30 years earlier. Unfortunately, he crashed in the first race, breaking a collarbone.

For 2002, the makeup of the official factory teams remained unchanged, but with the second generation 999-cc Testastretta engine available (with a 104-mm piston and an even shorter 58.8-mm stroke), the prospect of more Ducati dominance in World Superbike looked even more likely. The new engine will be even more powerful and will rev higher, and with both Bostrom and Xaus coming to terms with the 999, the Ducati triumvirate could prove unbeatable. In response to the dominance of the twins in this championship the minimum weight was increased to 361 pounds (164 kilograms), with 750-cc fours reduced to 317 pounds (159 kilograms). If nothing else, this demonstrated the absolute brilliance of the Desmoquattro design, which started out in World Superbike in 1988 with a weight advantage of 55 pounds (25 kilograms) and has been evolved to such a level that the 750-cc fours are totally outclassed. The Desmoquattro has been so dominant that it has virtually dictated the formula for success.

British Superbike Championship

Along with the AMA Superbike Championship, Ducati has always shown a strong interest in winning the British Superbike Championship. Much of this was due to the popularity of Superbike racing in Britain generated by British riders Carl Fogarty, and later Neil Hodgson. The success of the 916 in Britain began in 1995 when Steve Hislop won the British Superbike Championship, and Matt Llewellyn won the Shell Advance International Superbike Trophy. During 1996 Terry Rymer won five rounds on

From the outset, the 998 Testastretta proved competitive, and Bayliss provided consistent results that soon saw him comfortably leading the championship. Complementing Bayliss' performance was that of Bostrom. After a slow start, Bostrom absolutely dominated midseason, winning five

the Old Spice 955, but could only manage third in the championship. With two teams for 1997 the Ducatis also struggled. Supplied with 916 Racing machines were John Reynolds and Steve Hislop in the Reve Red Bull Team, and Sean Emmett in the GSE (Groundwork South East) team, but the Ducatis only managed three race wins.

Even though there was an expansion of racing support for 1998, the championship still eluded Ducati. Emmett was now riding alongside Reynolds in the Reve Red Bull Team, while Australian Troy Bayliss partnered Jamie Robertson in the GSE team. Llewellyn also rode for Red Bull, before replacing Robinson in the GSE line-up. It all came together in 1999 when Ducati Corse took a more active role and provided the two teams with new 996 RSs. Emmett and Reynolds stayed with Reve Red Bull, and former factory Ducati rider Neil Hodgson joined Bayliss in the INS/GSE team. Unlike previous seasons, the Ducatis dominated from the outset,

Bayliss narrowly going on to take the championship with seven victories.

Bayliss departed, initially to the AMA series, for 2000, and Niall McKenzie took his place alongside Hodgson in the INS/GSE team. James Haydon joined Reynolds in the Reve Red Bull Team and with updated specification 996 RSs, the Ducatis also were dominant this season. Hodgson ended up winning the championship, and moved back to World Superbike for 2001. The Ducatis were even more dominant in the 2001 championship. Updated 996 RSs were again provided to the Reve Red Bull team of Reynolds and Emmett, while Hislop rode for MonsterMob Ducati. Although both now veterans of the sport, Hislop and Reynolds were virtually unbeatable, fighting the championship to the end on their near identical machinery. After Hislop crashed at the penultimate round at Rockingham, Reynolds went on to comfortably take the championship.

Troy Bayliss served his apprenticeship in the British Superbike Championship on the GSE 996, winning in 1999. *Australian Motorcycle News*

Chapter Six

748

With the considerable development costs associated with implementing the production of the 916, it was inevitable that the model range would be expanded. Although there was the higher specification 916 SP and S during 1994, the first different displacement Desmoquattro was the smaller 748. Considering the engine started its life as a 748, and the cylinder heads were designed around a smaller bore, this wasn't surprising. Introduced for the 1995 model year there were initially three 748 versions, the Strada, Biposto, and Sport Production. Most 748s were Biposto, with the 748 SP specifically a Monoposto homologation machine for the expanding Supersport racing category. Although it was outlawed in the United States, in Europe the 748-cc twin was eligible to compete against 600-cc four-cylinder machines. Ducati hoped that just as the 916 twin was proving competitive with the 750-cc fours, the 748-cc twin could also beat the highly developed Japanese 600-cc fours.

Like the earlier prototype, the 748 shared its bore and stroke of 88x61.5 mm with the 750 F1 and Paso, as well as the current two-valve 750 Supersport. Unlike the 750 Supersport, which utilized the smaller crankcase Pantah five-speed engine block, the 748 was based on the larger six-speed crankcase engine of the 916. Essentially, the

748 was a smaller 916 Biposto, and consequently considerably overengineered. Not only were the crankcases identical, but the outside diameter of the cylinders was the same. Although there were new cylinder heads, with a slightly smaller combustion chamber to allow for the smaller pistons, the camshafts were identical to the 916 Biposto, as were the 33- and 29-mm valves. Also shared with the 916 Biposto was the Weber electronic injection system with a single injector per cylinder and a 1.6 M CPU, though the throttle body was reduced to 44 mm, in line with Supersport regulations. The crankshaft featured regular Macchi forged con-rods, with a lighter flywheel. There was no

748 (131 horsepower per liter) was the highest ever for a series-production Ducati engine until that time.

Just as with the 916, the frame was constructed of ALS 450 tubing, and it also provided for adjustment of the steering head angle. While the few Monoposto 748 Stradas produced in 1995 retained an aluminum rear subframe, the 748 Biposto shared its steel rear subframe with the 916 Biposto. The Showa suspension was also identical to that of the 916, the Biposto receiving a different rear unit to cope with the additional weight of a passenger. The 748 also shared its Brembo wheels and brakes with the 916, but used a lower profile front tire (120/60ZR17), a smaller (180/55ZR17) rear tire, and a narrower DID 520 VL4 (5/8x1/4-inch) drive chain. For a machine ostensibly identical to its larger brother, the less reciprocating internal engine weight and different power characteristics, along with the lower profile front and narrower rear tire, provided steering and handling that was arguably even superior to the 916's.

The 748 Sport Production

One of the more interesting new models for 1995 was the 748 Sport Production, though this wasn't as high a specification machine as the larger 916 Sport Production. In an era when all Desmoquattro Ducatis were red, what set the 748 SP apart was the striking yellow bodywork with its white number plate on the solo seat. Yellow first appeared on the U.S.-only 1992 900 Superlight, and this distinctive color would soon be associated with Ducati as much as red.

Unlike the 916 SP that featured a number of engine developments over the 916 Strada, the 748 SP's engine was little changed from the 748 Strada and Biposto. The compression ratio was slightly higher, at 11.6:1, and there were different camshafts. While the exhaust camshaft was the same as the 916 SP, there was a new inlet camshaft, this having timing figures similar to those of the 851 SP but with more valve lift (10.87 mm). Unlike the 916 SP that featured a P8 CPU with twin injectors per cylinder, the 748 SP shared its single injectors and 1.6 M CPU with the other 748s and 916 Biposto. Setting the 748 SP apart, though, were Pankl H-section steel con-rods, as fitted to the Senna and 1994 916 Strada. There was an external oil cooler, and with a 50-mm exhaust, the power was 104 horsepower at

For 1999 the 748 Biposto finally received improved front brakes, and the fork now featured the wider brake caliper mounts previously reserved for the 748 SPS. *Australian Motorcycle News*

external oil filter—reducing the oil capacity from 4 to 3 1/2 liters—and as the engine was designed to rev harder, the gearbox was the closer-ratio type of the 888 SP5. Third (28/20), fourth (26/22), fifth (24/23), and sixth gears (23/24) differed from those of the 916. The compression ratio was 11.5:1, and the exhaust system was 45 mm. Because it was basically a smaller 916, the 748 produced similar power to its larger brother, but at higher rpm. The lighter internal reciprocating parts also provided a more free-revving engine. With 98 horsepower at 11,000 rpm, the specific power output of the

11,000 rpm. In line with the projected racing nature of the 748 SP, an offset Woodruff key to alter the valve timing was located on the timing layshaft.

The 748 SP chassis, though, was more similar to the 916 SP, with an aluminum rear subframe and an upgraded Öhlins DU 3420 rear shock absorber. The front brakes were also from the 916 SP, with 320-mm fully floating cast-iron discs, stainless steel brake lines, and an adjustable brake lever. There were, however, no carbon-fiber body parts, but carbon-fiber Termignoni mufflers came with each machine. The 748 SP weighed 438 pounds (198 kilograms), and as the power output was similar to the regular 748, it didn't provide any more performance. If you wanted to race a 748 SP, Ducati provided a comprehensive racing uprating kit. Like the 916 SP, the 748 SP was also a reasonably limited edition motorcycle, and only 600 were produced during 1995.

Three uprating kits, two engine kits and one frame kit, were available for racing. Engine Kit No. 1 included lighter replacement engine parts, such as a clutch and alternator that could be installed without removing the engine from the frame. Engine Kit No. 2 was more comprehensive and included a lighter crankshaft and gearbox selector drum. The Frame Kit included a replacement fairing, seat, exhaust, injection unit supports, and modified wiring with a lighter generator.

There were only a few developments to the 748 SP for 1996. New crankcases appeared on all Desmoquattros, and the con-rods were the regular Macchi forged type rather than the Pankl H-section. There were four racing kits available this year, the more comprehensive engine kit including Pankl con-rods, and the two frame kits offering a wider range of lightweight components. Only 400 were built during 1996 and the specification was largely unchanged for 1997. The more comprehensive racing uprating kit for 1997 comprised only one engine and one frame kit, the engine kit including replacement valves and valve guides, along with a complete replacement gearbox. The 118-piece frame kit was much as before, and while the 748 SP was proving highly successful in Supersport racing, it was never as popular as a street bike. Thus, only 305 were manufactured during 1997.

The year 1996 was a very troubled one for production at Borgo Panigale, and demand far exceeded supply, so there were few changes to the 748 Biposto. The only changes were new crankcases and a sound-deadening clutch cover, and only 1,560 748s were produced this year. Apart from a few Monopostos for the French market, these were all red Bipostos, and they still weren't available in the United States. Following the Texas Pacific Group buy-out of Ducati in September 1996, there was an immediate

increase in production levels and an expansion of model offering. New for 1997 was the 748 S, in red or yellow, as a halfway model between the 748 Biposto and Sport Production. Initially this was projected as essentially a 748 SP (with an Öhlins shock absorber and fully floating cast-iron front brake discs) with a Biposto engine. When it finally appeared, however, the 748 S was basically a 748 Monoposto with all the standard Biposto components except for the aluminum rear subframe. This wasn't a particularly appealing formula, and only 100 were manufactured.

The 1997 748 Biposto was visually identical to the 1996 and 1995 version, but there were a small number of yellow versions available alongside the red. After three years, the 748 also finally made it to the United States, both as a Monoposto and Biposto. As if Ducati were testing the market to see if Americans would buy a premium priced 750, only a few were available, 240 Bipostos and 196 Monopostos. The U.S. specification 748 Monoposto in yellow may have looked like a European 748 SP, but like the earlier 888 SPO, the U.S. 748s had normal Strada engines. There was no external oil cooler, and the rear suspension was Showa.

The 748 SPS

Although the 748 SP had proved extremely successful in World Supersport racing, a change in the regulations allowing a 36.5-mm intake for the four-cylinder 600s altered the balance against the twins. Thus, there was a full racing specification 748 R available to selected teams for 1998. This didn't feature any street equipment, so the homologation version for Supersport racing was now the street 748 SPS (Sport Production Special). Replacing the 748 SP and looking outwardly similar, engine developments on the 748 SPS included the same forged titanium con-rods as used on the 1998 916 SPS, bronze valve guides, and revised valve rockers. The titanium con-rods were introduced to overcome the problem of con-rods breaking at 13,000 rpm. In order to improve racing performance, there were different intake tracts and throttle bodies, with the intake incorporated in the throttle body after the throttle valve. The intake was shortened to 33 mm, still with a 44-mm throttle body, with a machined internal finish. There was a new ignition pick-up designed for racing, and a modified voltage regulator. Unlike the 916 SPS, the 748 SPS retained the 2:1 (31/62) primary drive.

Most of the chassis developments were shared with the 916 SPS. These included a lighter 25CrMo4 frame, and new Showa fork with a wider brake caliper mount and different Brembo front brake calipers. There were also braided steel clutch and rear brake lines this year. As before, the front brake discs were fully floating cast-iron, and there was an Öhlins rear shock absorber. The weight of the 748 SPS was down slightly to 194 kilograms.

Only 570 748 SPSs were produced for 1998 and it remained a machine without a real purpose. Even with the optional engine and frame competition kit, the 748 SPS was no longer competitive in Supersport racing, and even fewer (204) were produced for 1999. A few were available for 2000, but this year the 748 SPS was superseded by the more sophisticated 748 R. Unlike the 1999 748, the 748 SPS continued virtually unchanged from 1998 but with different graphics. Thus, while all of the other Desmoquattros had a 520-watt triphase alternator, the 748 SPS retained the earlier, and lighter, 350-watt alternator. Although the 996 SPS went to steel brake discs in 1999, the 748 SPS retained the fully floating cast-iron type; it was the final production Ducati with these brakes.

Racing 748s: The 748 Racing and Racing Special

In World Supersport racing, the 748 SP had proved surprisingly successful, and with the expansion of the profile of this series, 20 748 Racing machines were made available to selected teams for 1998. Assembled in the racing department, World Supersport regulations limited modifications, and the 748 Racing wasn't quite as exotic as the 916 Racing. It retained the single-injector I.A.W. 1.6 M CPU and was basically a fully race kitted 748 SPS. The gearbox was from the 916 Racing, there was a stronger clutch with sintered clutch plates with stiffer springs, and nimonic valves in stock sizes of 33 and 29 mm. Weight-saving measures extended to a lighter clutch cover, and a 180-watt alternator. Shorter (33-mm) carbon-fiber inlet manifolds, homologated through the 748 SPS, were incorporated as part of the throttle body after the throttle valve. There was a 916 Racing cooling system, and a racing exhaust with carbon-fiber mufflers. With quite restrictive regulations, the power of the 748 Racing was increased only slightly over the 748 SP and SPS to 108 horsepower at 11,500 rpm.

Regulations allowed more latitude in the modification of the chassis, and here, full

Replacing the 748 SP for 1998 was the 748 SPS. This remained in production through 1999. Here is a 1999 model—1998 versions didn't feature tank decals. *Ian Falloon*

Fabrizio Pirovano rode this race-kitted 748 SP to victory in the 1996 Open Supersport Championship. Its success ultimately led to the factory releasing official 748 racers. *Australian Motorcycle News*

racing equipment was specified. This included complete carbon-fiber bodywork, sump guard, chain guard and mufflers, front dashboard, and electronic control unit mount. There was racing-only wiring and instrumentation. As a result of all these modifications, the weight was down to 376 pounds (170 kilograms). For the 1999 season, 18 748 Racing machines were produced, very similar to those of 1998 but incorporated the revised fairing and tank of the 748 SPS that year.

Even with all the improvements, the 748 Racing failed to deliver the World Supersport title in 1998 and 1999, so for the 2000 season Ducati Corse produced a considerably higher specification 748 RS (Racing Special). Based on the new production 748 R (replacing the 748 SPS), this featured a newly homologated frame and airbox and an injection system similar to that of the 996 Factory racer. A single Marelli IWP 069 injector was placed above the throttle valve, with the throttle body inside the airbox and very short intake ducts. World Supersport regulations required that the injection system be the same I.A.W. 1.6 M system as the street 748 R, rather than the MF3-S system of the 996 Factory. Regulations allowed, however, for an increase in throttle body diameter to 54 mm. There were also a number of engine developments, including

new camshafts with more duration than the 748 R, a 12:1 compression ratio, Menon chrome-topped racing 36-mm and 30-mm valves, a closer ratio gearbox, and a 1 3/4-pound (0.78 kilogram) lighter flywheel. Ostensibly the 748 RS was a full racing bike, right down to the new water pump and larger radiator, and wider (19-mm) exposed cam belts and new pulleys. With the 54-mm racing titanium Termignoni exhaust system, the power was an impressive 124 horsepower at 12,000 rpm.

World Supersport regulations required that the chassis also be production based, so the chassis specifications were the same as the 748 R, except for a new generation Mark II Öhlins shock absorber with internal bleeds and a one-piece rear wheel nut. The 748 RS also had a different electrical system, with a triphase 280-watt alternator. On paper and on the track, the 748 RS promised much, and 52 were produced for 2000. Even though Ducati Corse appeared to lose interest in pursuing the World Supersport Championship, a further batch of 42 748 RS were produced for 2001. Apart from the updated Öhlins forks and Brembo brakes of the production 748 R, these were ostensibly the same as those of the previous year.

Except for new logos, only on the fairing and not the fuel tank, there were few changes to the 748 Strada for the 1998 model year. Finally, there were adjustable clutch and brake levers, and also a new regulator. Developments to the engine included Kevlar-reinforced timing belts from the racing versions. Yellow 748 Bipostos were now available alongside red, and there was a limited edition 748 L available only in the United States. One hundred of these silver 748 Ls were sold through the Neiman Marcus mail order catalog at a premium price. Essentially the 748 L was a stock 748 Biposto with a carbon-fiber front mudguard and chainguard. A Donna Karan New York leather jacket and Dainese gloves were also included with each 748 L.

Although still not especially popular in the United States, by 1998 the 748 accounted for nearly 40 percent of Desmoquattro production. Ducati manufactured 3,491 that year, of which, only 450 went to the United States. For 1999, the family designation became Superbike (rather than Hypersport), and as the 916 became the 996, the 748 received many of the trickle-

down improvements. Unlike the 748 SPS, the 748 now had a 520-watt triphase alternator that allowed for the high and low beam of the headlights to be run simultaneously. There were new three-spoke Brembo wheels, constructed of GA/Si7 with less silicon content than before, reducing rim weight. The Showa front forks also had a wider front brake caliper mount (like the 1998 748 and 916 SPS), and there was a completely revised braking system that included a racing-inspired PSC 16-mm master cylinder and braided steel brake lines. The clutch master cylinder was now a PSC 13 mm, with a stainless steel line and preassembled piston. There were also new stainless steel semifloating 320-mm front brake discs with aluminum carriers, the 4-mm discs slightly thinner than those of the 996. At the rear was a Brembo P 32 G brake caliper, contributing to an improved braking system. A new fairing, fuel tank, and revised twin-bolt handlebar mount completed the small upgrades for 1999.

For some reason, though demand for the 748 reached a hiatus during 1999, and with production reduced to 2,228 machines (24 percent of Superbike production), the future of the smaller model was in some doubt. However, instead of axing the 748, Ducati expanded the model range for 2000 to three

models. This had the desired effect, not only saving the 748, but resulting in a soar in demand. During the year 2000, production of the 748 line-up was 7,791, over 50 percent more than that of the 996 that year.

Central to the new lease on life for the 748 was the creation of a base model, the 748 Economico, offering virtually identical specification to its more expensive brethren. All 748s for 2000 received a number of developments, including a new metal head gasket and cylinder assembly, thicker crankshaft shims, and larger crankshaft bearing bushings. To match these larger bearing bushings were a new pair of timing gears. Other developments included a modified flywheel to accommodate a new bushing on the starter clutch gear and a new oil pressure switch with modified calibration. New engine cases with a closed by-pass hole completed this new specification, which was in total much as before, including the same camshafts, valves, and 31/62 primary drive. New for 2000 were 50-mm throttle bodies from the 996, and the power was 97 horsepower at 11,000 rpm.

To keep the price down the chassis featured a number of economies. The bronze-painted frame no longer featured an eccentric adjustment to alter the steering head angle, which was now fixed at 24.5 degrees, with

Marchesini wheels elevated the 748 S (in the foreground) above the 748 Economico (background). The 748 S was also available as a Monoposto. *Ian Falloon*

were improved, with 320x5-mm stainless steel front discs, and a PSC 16-mm master cylinder.

Further budget considerations were apparent in the fairing fasteners, now no longer the quick release Dzus-type, while the flange at the bottom of the fuel tank no longer incorporated quick release fittings. A smaller PS 12-mm clutch master cylinder, a new kickstand with safety sensor and safety relay, and new wiring completed the upgraded specification for 2000. The smaller clutch master cylinder was to improve the hydraulic leverage ratio and reduce muscular effort, while the automatically retracting kickstand had long been criticized. The 748 Economico was only available as a Biposto, in either red or yellow, and weighed slightly less than the earlier 748, at 433 pounds (196 kilograms).

The 748 R

The 748 R replaced the 748 SPS as a Supersport homologation machine for 2000. In an effort to wrestle back the World Supersport trophy, Ducati made the 748R the highest specification Desmoquattro ever. Incorporating many features from the World Superbike racers, the 748 R was a race replica in the tradition of the finest Ducati sportbikes. Central to the 748 R's specification was the incorporation of the "Kyalami" frame that had proved so

97 mm of trail. A regular 43-mm Showa GD 131 fork with chrome-plated rather than titanium-nitrided fork legs was fitted, and at the rear was an adjustable Sachs-Boge shock absorber. The wheels on the 748 Economico were the bronze-painted three-spoke Brembo wheels of earlier models. The front brakes

The 748 R was the highest specification production Ducati available for 2000 and was the only model to feature a single shower injector with a larger airbox. *Ian Falloon*

successful on the World Superbike racer during 1998. Only previously available in the 1998 British market 916 SPS Fogarty Replica, with the 748 R this important development became more widely available. Unlike the Fogarty Replica, the 748 R also took advantage of the larger airbox. This was increased from 8 to 14 liters and was designed to not only provide cooler air, but a low-frequency pulse to broaden the power band. The larger, 54-mm throttle body was incorporated inside the airbox, and was also 67 mm shorter with new funnels. Above the butterflies was a single "shower form" injector, and the injection system was the same Weber 1.6 M.

Central to the 748 R was an engine based on the 996, with stronger crankcases with reversed bolts, bigger port cylinder heads, and 36- and 30-mm valves. There were metal cylinder head gaskets, thicker crankshaft shims, larger crankshaft bushings, new timing gears, and a modified flywheel. The oil pump, borrowed from the 996 SPS, featured a built-in by-pass. There was a larger diameter bushing for the fixed belt roller and higher quality timing belts, now 19 mm wide rather than 17 mm. The 748 R also included the highest lift camshafts ever fitted to a production four-valve Ducati, 12.5 mm on the inlet and 10.5 mm on the exhaust. These camshafts also featured revised timing, now derived from the 996 Racing but with closer cam phasing and reduced overlap to reduce exhaust emissions. The valves also had a reduced valve center distance, so there were new valve rockers with stronger valve closing springs. As with the Ducati Corse 996, the combustion chambers on the 748 R were machines with extremely high precision CNC equipment. The 31/62 primary drive was as before, as was the gearbox, but the 748 R now had the 520-watt triphase alternator, along with a new crankshaft and alternator cover. There was also a racing slipper clutch, and the 748 R remained the only production Ducati with this, even after the release of the 996 R for 2001. With a new Termignoni exhaust system, the 748 R produced the same 106 horsepower as the earlier 748 SPS, but at a lower 11,000 rpm. The smoother and more progressive torque curve was more important in reducing lap times.

The rest of the chassis was much the same as the 748 S. Both the frame and five-spoke Marchesini wheels were painted

Specification upgrades for 2001 saw the 748 R receive the same Öhlins fork and Brembo brakes as the new 996 R. *Ian Falloon*

"gunmetal gray," and the Showa forks featured low friction gold-colored TiN-coated fork legs. There was the new nonself-retracting kickstand, and a Brembo PSC-12 mm clutch master cylinder. The braking system also came from 996, with Toshiba TT 2802 sintered front brake pads and 320x5-mm stainless steel front discs. There was a PSC 16-mm master cylinder, but the 748 R now had a Showa, rather than an Öhlins, rear shock absorber. Available in yellow only, and as a Monoposto, the 424-pound (192-kilogram) 748 R was undoubtedly one of the

most exciting production Ducatis ever offered, up to that time.

As with the earlier 748 SP and SPS, a racing kit was also available for the 748 R. This consisted of a complete Termignoni exhaust system and a replacement EPROM, to provide an immediate increase of 6 horsepower, to 112 horsepower. While still not eligible for Supersport racing in the United States, the 748 R proved eminently suitable for the AMA Pro Thunder Championship. In the Pro Thunder race at Daytona in March 2000, Shawn Conrad took first place on a 748 R, with Jeff Nash second. Nash won the 2001 Daytona Supertwins race on an Edo Vigna-prepared 748 R.

For 2001 there were only moderate developments to the production 748 R, all intended to enhance racing performance, though the power was unchanged. There was a lighter flywheel, with the crankshaft now balanced with tungsten inserts for improved power response. The tungsten plugs were heavier than steel, but were designed to offset the more compact, sharp profile crank webs. There were also lighter pistons and titanium valve cotters, providing quicker

engine response and higher rpm. To improve gear selection there was a lighter vacuum precision-cast desmodromic gear selector drum, providing more accurate gear shifting. Completing the list of upgrades were a carbon-fiber airbox, and 996 gearbox ratios, with a lower (26/22) fourth gear. All the other ratios were unchanged, though all 748s still used the 2:1 primary drive.

For 2001 the 748 R frame was lighter, and constructed of 1.5-mm-thick chrome-molybdenum tubing. The design was similar to that of the new 996 R, as was the suspension and brakes. There were the racing-specification Öhlins 43-mm upside-down forks with TiN-coated stanchions, along with a racing Öhlins rear shock absorber. The front Brembo braking system also was more racing oriented, with thinner 320x4.5-mm discs with nine floating fasteners and lightweight ergal carriers. The discs weighed 400 grams less than before, and there were new racing-inspired Brembo calipers with four 34-mm pistons and four individual pads. Also shared with the 996 R was the 15-mm front master cylinder. Although only available in yellow in the United States, elsewhere the

748 R was also available in red, and also received a numbered plaque on the top triple clamp. The only chassis component inferior to the 996 was the Boge steering damper, though U.S. versions received an Öhlins, providing even better value. For the 2002 model year, the 996 R was essentially unchanged except for the smoother 996 R fairing and revised decals.

Filling out the 748 line-up for 2000 was the 748 S. In a choice of red or yellow, and Monoposto or Biposto, this was really a development of the 1999 748. The engine was the same as the 748 Economico, also without an external oil cooler, and the gunmetal gray frame still offered adjustable steering head angle. There were five-spoke aluminum Marchesini wheels, 500 grams lighter than the three-spoke Brembo, and the 43-mm Showa GD 131 forks featured gold titanium-nitrided (TiN) fork legs with superior surface hardening. There was also the Showa shock absorber of the earlier 748.

There were only detail alterations to the 748 line-up for the 2001 model year. These included a sealed-for-life battery, and an improved clutch slave cylinder. All the engine mounts were increased from 10 to 12 mm for greater rigidity, and the fourth gear ratio lowered slightly. For the first time all Desmoquattro Superbikes shared the same gearbox ratios. The highly successful 748 Economico now had a "gunmetal gray" frame and wheels so visually there was little to separate the 748 with the 748 S, apart from the TiN-coated Showa fork stanchions, Showa shock absorber, and Marchesini wheels. By the 2002 model year the 748 was the only Ducati Superbike to retain the earlier Desmoquattro engine. While the 998 went to the new 5.9 M CPU, the 748 retained the earlier 1.6 M type. All 748s now sported the aerodynamically superior smooth fairing from the 2001 996 R and slightly revised decals, with the 748 S now also available in titanium gray with red wheels. In all other respects,

Fabrizio Pirovano rode the Team Alstare 748 SP to victory in the 1996 Open Supersport Championship and carried the Number One plate for 1997.
Ian Falloon

the 748 was unchanged, and, as before, U.S. versions were also available as Monoposto.

While the 748 may have appeared to be a shrunken 916 and the poor relation in the Desmoquattro family, it has always provided exceptional value. Production costs are very similar between the 748 and 916/996, yet 748s have been sold with a significantly smaller price tag than the larger versions. Considering they provide similar outright performance to a 916, albeit with markedly different power characteristics, the 748 could be the pick of Desmoquattro line-up. A 748 gives the rider a different experience. Rather than tractor-like torque, here is an engine that thrives on revs and emits an intoxicating sound. With arguably superior handling, the 748 can stand alone beyond the shadow of the 996 as one of Ducati's finest.

World Supersport

Right from the outset the 748 SP was a force in the fledgling European Supersport Championship of 1995, held as support races to World Superbike. The Belgian rider

Michael Paquay won seven of the eight races on the Team Alstare 748 SP, taking victory in the championship. Serafino Foti came in second on another 748 SP. For 1995 the 750-cc twins received a weight advantage over the fours, but for 1996, all machines needed to weigh in at 380 pounds (172 kilograms). Few modifications were allowed and the engines had to retain the stock camshafts, valve sizes, and airbox shape. The brakes, wheels, and suspension also had to be the same as the production version.

For the 1996 Open Supersport Championship, Fabrizio Pirovano rode and also dominated, the Team Alstare 748 SP, winning five races. The engine now produced 115 horsepower at 11,800 rpm. The series earned world status for 1997 with the establishment of the Supersport World Cup, and again, the 748 SP won the championship. Although suffering many electrical problems, Paolo Casoli won the title on the Gio.Ca.Moto entry. This year, the power was up to 120 horsepower, at the crankshaft, at 12,000 rpm.

Ruben Xaus spent an apprenticeship year on the Team Ducati Infostrada 748 RS during 2000 before moving to World Superbike. *Ian Falloon*

The success of Daniele Casolari's Gio.Ca.Moto team during 1997, along with Gio.Ca.Moto's new association with Ducati Motor, saw the formation of Team Ducati Performance for 1998. Paolo Casoli rode the factory 748 Racing in the Supersport World Series, but his results were disappointing. Altered regulations now tipped the balance toward the four-cylinder machines, and Casoli complained that the 1998 bike was too slow. He could only manage fourth overall in the Supersport World Series, although he won two races. The Ducati Performance 748 produced 117 horsepower at the rear wheel, and weighed right on the 172 kilogram minimum.

For 1999 the series became the World Supersport Championship, and Ducati Performance again entered Paolo Casoli on its 748. This year the 748 was totally outclassed, and with Casoli missing much of the season through injury, he could only manage 14th in the championship. This led to the release of the production 748 R and racing 748 RS for 2000. Two 748 RSs were run alongside the World Superbike machines in the Team Ducati Infostrada. Paolo Casoli again rode the 748, joined by the 22-year-old Spanish rider, Ruben Xaus. Pietro di Gianesin prepared the engines, and immediately the 748 RS was more competitive. Casoli won at Monza and at Brands Hatch, and Xaus at Assen, with Casoli finishing a close second in the championship. Ducati Corse decided to concentrate on World Superbike for 2001, but continued to provide support to the Dienza team of Vittoriano Guareschi and Dean Thomas. Without full factory support, though, the 748 RSs were swamped by the sea of Japanese four-cylinder 600s. The 748 RS was obviously close to the end of its competitive life, but since 1995 it had proved the only twin-cylinder 750 to mount any challenge to the 600-cc four-cylinder machines.

With Ducati Corse not fully supporting a World Supersport entry for 2001, the leading Ducati 748 RS was Vittoriano Guareschi on the Dienza machine. *Ian Falloon*

Chapter Seven

996

As the factory World Superbike racers had been running 996-cc engines since 1996, it was inevitable that the production 916 would eventually grow to a full 996-cc. There also was more competition in the market, with Honda, Suzuki, and Aprilia all offering 1,000-cc V-twins. Now, essentially unchanged since 1994, for the 916 to retain its position as the leading twin-cylinder sportsbike, it needed more displacement. This occurred for the 1999 model year, when the generic 996 replaced the 916, with the family terminology changing to Superbike (from Hypersport).

The 996 also exemplified several years of development, so there was more to the new model than simply a displacement increase. Now derived from the 916 SPS, the 996 engine featured stronger crankcases with a wider stud pattern to allow for the 98-mm pistons and reversed bolts for extra strength. Also from the 916 SPS came larger valves, 36-mm inlet and 30-mm exhaust, and higher-ratio primary drive gears (32/59). The 996 received a higher tensile strength crankshaft, and a new clutch basket and clutch actuation system. The clutch consisted of eight driven plates seven flat and one spring, and seven driving plates. There were larger crankshaft bearing shells and thicker crankshaft shims, but unlike those on the SPS, the con-rods were still the Macchi forged steel type.

In many respects the 996 was a carryover from the 916. Both models shared relatively mild desmodromic camshafts, gearbox ratios, and 1.6 M Weber injection system. Known as the 1.6 M.B1 and still with one engine sensor, this was developed to incorporate twin injectors per cylinder. As the 1.6 M was primarily a single point injection system, both the injectors were triggered simultaneously, unlike the sequential triggering of the P8 system. There was a new 074 EPROM, and as in the past, U.S. versions received slightly different mapping. The 996 also received a more powerful 520-watt triphase alternator, along with a new alternator cover. This alternator allowed for a more powerful headlamp, and the running of high and low beams simultaneously so that on low beam both headlights were operating.

One area that had been continually developed through the racing program was the intake and exhaust system. The airbox for the 996 featured improved sealing, and there were shorter venturi-shaped intakes, but there was also a reducer in the air filter outlet. The exhaust header pipes were oval-section and the exhaust diameter was 45 mm. Along with larger volume, 120x420-mm mufflers, the power output was a conservative 112 horsepower at a moderate 8,500 rpm. The 996's emphasis was still on midrange rather than peak power. It seemed strange that the

While the 996 looked outwardly similar to the 1998 916, there was more to the new model than simply a larger engine. *Australian Motorcycle News*

996 was in such a moderate state of tune,
as all the competitive 1,000-cc twins were
more powerful, but for those wanting more
power there was always the 996 SPS. Even
though the design was now over six years
old, the 996 chassis still provided class-
leading handling.

Most chassis development concerned the
front brakes, suspension, and wheels. As with
the 1998 916 SPS, the Showa front forks
had sliders that provided a wider mount for
the new Brembo brake calipers. These were
claimed to increase caliper rigidity, and the
calipers featured revised internal plumbing.
Braking performance was also improved
through sintered Toshiba TT 2802 brake pads
and a PSC 16-mm front master cylinder
derived from the Brembo racing radial type.
The PSC 13-mm clutch master cylinder was
also a new generation. Finally, the thin
stainless steel discs of the 916 made way for
thicker 320x5-mm semifloating stainless steel
discs with steel studs on the flanges.
Completing the upgraded braking specification

were stainless steel brake lines. Finally, one of
the criticisms leveled at the 916 since its
inception was addressed, and the 996 brakes
were fully up to the task. There was also a
stainless steel clutch line, preassembled with
the piston to ensure air-free operation.
Upgraded too was the rear braking system
with a stainless steel brake line and a new
Brembo P 32 G brake caliper. Also new were
the three-spoke Brembo wheels, now
constructed of GA/Si7 with a lower silicon
content to reduce weight, although the sizes
of 3.50x17 inches and 5.50x17 inches were
unchanged. Other chassis developments
included a new fairing and fuel tank with new
decals, two-bolt handlebar mounts, and a
revised seat mount. The 996 also weighed
less than its predecessor, at 438 pounds
(198 kilograms) dry.

As with the 916, the 996 was generally
a Biposto, though the United States received
Biposto and Monoposto versions, in yellow
and red. Also only for the United States, and
specifically for California, was a hybrid 996

S (Special). The specification was along the lines of the earlier 888 SPO and took the chassis of the 996 SPS with the regular 112-horsepower 996 engine. The specification included an Öhlins rear shock absorber and steering damper, and Marchesini five-spoke wheels; it was only a red Monoposto but without an aluminum rear subframe. There were a number of carbon-fiber body parts, and a numbered plaque on the top triple clamp, but though the 996 S looked to be an SPS, it wasn't quite as exotic. The creation of the 996 provided the largest Desmoquattro with a new lease of life, with the total production of the 996 series up to 6,929 units for 1999.

The 996 SPS

Endemic to Ducati's marketing policy since the Texas Pacific Group takeover has been an annual upgrading of the specification of the entire line-up. None has exemplified this more than the range-leading 996 SPS, and every new version of this magnificent motorcycle has represented an improvement over the previous model. For 1999, many of the features of the limited production 1998 916 SPS Fogarty Replica filtered through to the 996 SPS, though the frame was still the earlier type.

While the general engine specifications were unchanged, new for the 1999 996 SPS were the 520-watt triphase alternator, a new oil pump with a 25/40 ratio, and a different oil delivery pipe to the cylinder heads. There was a second lubrication circuit delivering oil to the vertical cylinder through a hole in a casing screw to help cool the piston crown. The 996 SPS retained the forged titanium con-rods and the P8 injection system for the twin injectors, and unlike the 996, there was no air flow reducer in the airbox. The 996 SPS featured a different clutch to the 996, with 10 driven plates (eight flat, two spring) and eight driving plates. Setting the 996 SPS apart from the 996 for 1999 were five-spoke Marchesini wheels. These were patterned on

the type used by the factory racers and weighed around 17.5 ounces (500 grams) less than the new three-spoke Brembo. First appearing on the U.K-only Fogarty Replica, they retained the sizes of 3.50x17 inches and 5.50x17 inches. The front braking system was identical to that of the 996, with the 320x5-mm stainless steel discs replacing the earlier fully floating cast-iron type. Still with an Öhlins rear shock absorber and steering damper, each red 996 SPS came with a small plaque on the top triple clamp. Production was down to 658 for 1999, of which 56 came to the United States. Later in 1999, there was a second series of the 996 SPS produced to homologate new cylinder heads for the World Superbike program. Except for the cylinder heads in a different alloy, these were identical and were known as the 996 SPS 2. Only 150 of this second series of 996 SPS were produced.

As expected, the 996 SPS was upgraded yet again for 2000. The engine specifications were as before, but for a modified flywheel to accommodate a new bushing on the starter clutch gear and a new oil pressure switch with revised calibration. With 2000 the final

Continual upgrading of the SPS saw it receive an Öhlins front fork for 2000.
Ian Falloon

year for the 996 SPS engine with the P8 injection system, it was the chassis that received the most development. Shared with the 996 were the non-retracting kickstand, PS 12-mm clutch master cylinder, new wiring, and Ducati Corse tachometer, but elevating the 996 SPS were a 43-mm Öhlins front fork and a "sealed-for-life" battery. The battery saved 2.4 pounds (1.1 kilograms), contributing to a reduction in overall weight to 413 pounds (187 kilograms). The frame and wheels were also gunmetal gray this year.

The Öhlins fork featured gold TiN-coated fork legs, and included some developments from the World Superbike Ducati Corse 996. There were stiffer triple clamps, 85-mm steering lugs, and the axle mounting height was reduced from 110 to 80 mm. This increased the extension of the fork stanchions and provided more precise front end control. They also provided less front wheel travel of 120 mm. The rear subframe was 1.1 pounds (0.5 kilograms) lighter and constructed of aluminum tubing with the same cross-section as the factory racers. As a result, the 996 SPS retained its position as

the premier sporting twin. For the 2001 model year, the 996 SPS was replaced by the next generation 996 R, but the 123-horsepower engine lived on in the European specification 996 S.

There were only detail improvements to the 996 for the 2000 model year. A modified flywheel accommodated a new bushing on the starter clutch gear, and from the 996 SPS came new oil pipes to cylinder heads. Also from the 996 SPS were gunmetal gray five-spoke Marchesini wheels, and from the Factory Replica came Showa forks with gold TiN-coated fork legs. There was a PS 12-mm clutch master cylinder, new wiring, Ducati Corse tachometer, and kickstand with a safety sensor. As before, the 996 was available in either Biposto or Monoposto, and in red or yellow. Again specifically for the United States was the 996 S, still essentially a standard 996 engine in a 996 SPS running gear. Only a red Monoposto, this year there was an aluminum rear subframe, and while there was an Öhlins shock absorber, the fork was a 43-mm Showa. Production numbered only 200.

There were few changes for 2001, although the visually similar 996 S provided SPS performance. *Ian Falloon*

101

The 1999 Factory Replica was the second series of replica 996 SPSs, and the first model to feature the gold TiN-coated forks. The decals were patterned on Fogarty's World Superbike racer. *Ian Falloon*

There were no factory replica decals on the 2000 model Factory Replica 2 Pista as it left the factory, but there were some revised engine parts for Superbike homologation. *Ian Falloon*

An expansion of the 996 range for the 2001 model year saw three models, with the 123-horsepower 996 SPS engine powering the new 996 S. There were only small changes to the 996, and a closer-ratio gearbox was standardized throughout the Desmoquattro Superbike range. All the ratios were the same as the earlier 996 SPS but for a slightly lower (26/20 instead of 26/22) fourth gear. The 996s also now featured an Öhlins rear suspension unit, a sealed-for-life battery, and a new Brembo clutch slave cylinder.

Slotting in above the 996 in the line-up was the 996 S. Looking visually identical to the 996, European versions had a 996 SPS-specification engine, and U.S. versions retained the 112-horsepower 996 unit. European 996 Ss were Monoposto or Biposto, and U.S. models were Monoposto only. They also came with an Öhlins (rather than Boge) steering damper and some carbon-fiber body parts. The 996 S frame had a steel rear subframe and the suspension included a TiN-coated 43-mm Showa fork with an Öhlins rear suspension unit. There were some modifications to the 996 SPS engine in its transformation into the European 996 S. After soldiering on since 1993, the P8 injection system finally bit the dust, and the 996 S used the 1.6 M B1 twin simultaneous injector setup of the 996. These were now positioned inside the 50-mm throttle bodies. In other respects the engine specifications were the same as the 996 SPS, including the titanium con-rods. Considering the 996 S was sold at a discounted price, compared to the 996 SPS, it represented remarkable value for money. In England, the 998 S was also offered as a

Hodgson Replica from August 2001. It was painted in the orange GSE colors, and its engine developments, including a 54-mm Termignoni exhaust system, yielded 130 horsepower. A carbon-fiber kit that set the Hodgson Replica apart included a complete airbox and air intake setup, swingarm cover, sprocket cover, and alloy rear seat footpegs. However, 2001 was to be the final year for the 996 Superbike. For 2002, all large displacement models carried the new Testastretta engine, with the previous 996-cc engine only living on in the ST4S.

Limited Edition 996 SPSs:
The Factory Replica and Pista

Even though the 996 SPS was already a limited production motorcycle, the release of a small number of 916 SPS Fogarty Replicas in 1998 to homologate the new racing frame began a trend. These machines were only available in England, but soon the rest of the world wanted them too. Therefore, during 1999 another series of 996 SPS Factory Replicas were produced, this time only numbering 150.

Available in Europe, Japan, and Australia, these were ostensibly 996 SPSs with decals patterned on Fogarty's Ducati Performance World Superbike racer. This time the frame was a standard 996 SPS and while the 43-mm Showa fork was from the 996 SPS the 1999 Factory Replica was the first to feature the gold-colored TiN-coated fork stanchions. As demand exceeded supply, there was a further batch of 996 SPS Factory Replicas for 2000. Though originally these were to be the 996 SPS 3, they were officially titled the 996 Factory Replica 2, and known as the "Pista," or, circuit.

The purpose of these small runs of Factory Replicas was to homologate new parts for the World Superbike racing program, and the Pista wore new cylinder heads with more material around the studs to improve stiffness and solve head gasket sealing problems. The rest of the specification was the same as the 2000 model year 996 SPS. To differentiate it from the previous Factory Replica there was tricolor striping on the fairing and seat, a special numbered plaque, and a 2000 Team Ducati Infostrada decal kit. A total of 149 of the 996 SPS Pistas were produced, and these were the last of the 996 SPS, the end of a magnificent line that had its origins in the 851 SP2 of 1990.

Although ostensibly a 996 SPS, the Pista had specific decals and a separate numbered sequence.
Ian Falloon

Chapter Eight

ST4, ST4S and Monster S4

Just as the continual evolution of the Desmoquattro engine has been crucial to its success, so has the expansion of the range of motorcycles receiving this power unit. Ducati's product strategy took a massive leap forward in 1992 with the creation of the Monster, an entirely new concept in naked motorcycles. This used the venerable two-valve engine from the Supersport, first in 900-cc and then in 750- and 600-cc versions, and it has provided Ducati with unprecedented sales success. Sport touring motorcycles have historically also been important for Ducati, and after some delay the sport touring ST2 was released for 1998, with a new 944-cc liquid-cooled two-valve engine. As both these designs could be adapted for the four-valve Desmoquattro engine, it was inevitable that four-valve Sport Touring and Monsters would appear at some stage, but it took some time for them to eventuate.

Both the Monster and ST2 differed from the 916 and 748 in that they weren't creations of Massimo Tamburini and his Cagiva Research Center in San Marino, but of Miguel Galluzzi at Cagiva Morrazone in Varese. Thus the concept and execution were quite different in a number of areas, and both were more in the older Ducati tradition of utilizing existing components from other production models. Both the Monster and

Sport Touring drew on other designs and were amalgams of several models, so their incubation period was also considerably shorter than that of the 916.

Galluzzi's first effort for Ducati was the Monster, and it was an original and inspired design concept. So successful has the Monster been that by 2001, a total of 100,000 had been produced, and they were the mainstay for the company during the 1990s. Because the two-valve Monster was so successful, and Desmoquattro engine production was well utilized, Ducati didn't feel the need to create a four-valve version until the 2001 model year. Less popular was the Sport Touring 2. As a narrower focus motorcycle, and one without the benefit of the cult status the Monster enjoyed, only 7,474 ST2s were produced between 1996 and 2000.

Unlike the Monster, the first Sport Touring prototype used the 916-cc Desmoquattro engine rather than the eventual production two-valve unit. Back in 1995, while Ducati was still under the Cagiva regime and struggling to meet production targets, three ST4s with 916-cc Desmoquattro engines were constructed. However, as the production of 916-cc engines was stretched to the limit, meeting the demand for the 916, the Sport Touring 916 was shelved and replaced by the ST2. Even then, production was delayed due

When released for the 1999 model year, the ST4 looked visually identical to the ST2. *Ian Falloon*

to the problems of 1996 and only four 944-cc ST2s and one 916-cc ST4 were produced during 1996. It wasn't until the Texas Pacific Group buyout in September 1996 that production of the Sport Touring series could commence. Although it had been ready for some time, the ST2 finally made the production line during 1997, and was the first new model to appear under the TPG administration. Because the Sport Touring design was originally conceived with the four-valve engine, it was no surprise when the ST4 was released for the 1999 model year. During 1997, three more test machines were constructed, and the series was in production by July 1998.

The ST2 had a commendable liquid-cooled two-valve engine that produced 83 horsepower from its 944-cc (94x68-mm) displacement. Although the ST2 provided acceptable performance, the chassis always cried out for the more powerful four-valve engine. And when the top-of-the-line 916 Hypersport grew to a full 996 cc, the Sport Touring series was the perfect recipient for the smaller engine. However, when it came to adapting the 94x66-mm 916-cc Desmoquattro to the ST4, it wasn't simply a matter of swapping engines. Ducati's engineers felt that it was important to maintain the same weight distribution, with the engine in the same position in the chassis. As the Desmoquattro engine was longer than the two-valve unit, the front cylinder head was shortened to maintain adequate front wheel clearance with the 24-degree steering head angle. This required moving the exhaust camshaft 10 mm closer to the center of the engine, still providing 49 percent of weight on the front wheel. The general specifications, though, were unchanged when the engine made the transition into the ST4. The valve sizes were 33 and 29 mm, and the camshafts gave identical timing and valve lift to the 916. Although there was the new primary drive ratio of 32/59 (1.84:1), the clutch and six-speed gearbox were also from the 916. The Weber Marelli injector system was the 1.6 M with a single injector per cylinder, but unlike the 916, the ST had a separate airbox that wasn't intrinsic with the frame structure. The exhaust system also was similar to that of the ST2, though this was redesigned for the ST4. There was a redesigned water pump,

and it shared with other 1999 models the upgraded electrical system that included a new triphase 520-watt alternator instead of the ST2's 420-watt type. Completing the ST4 specification was a small black, curved, oil radiator underneath the front cylinder. With an 11:1 compression ratio, the power was 107 horsepower at 9,000 rpm. This was more than enough to provide the ST4 with the performance expected of a European sport touring motorcycle par excellence. The engine was noticeably smoother and more responsive than that of the ST2 and only suffered in comparison by not having the same tractor-like torque at low engine speeds.

The general chassis specifications of the ST4 were the same as the ST2. Unlike the 916, the Sport Touring series utilized a tubular steel frame derived from the Monster, which was based on the earlier 888. This frame didn't feature a lower engine support, and the dual-sided steel swingarm pivoted solely on the engine cases. The frame was constructed in ALS 450, with a 55-mm diameter steering head tube positioned to provide a relatively steep steering head angle of 24 degrees. With the trail of 102 mm and a moderate wheelbase of 55.8 inches (1,430 mm), the Sport Touring provided agile, yet stable steering and handling. Where the Sport Touring differed from both the Monster and 888 was the monoshock linkage that was patterned after the 916 system. There was a central rod with two ball joints, but the set length of 272 mm was a little longer than the 261 mm of the 916. As with the 916, this rod length could be adjusted to provide a different ride height.

Also departing from the Monster with its Supersport-derived front brakes and suspension was the Sport Touring's 916-type Showa suspension and new-generation Brembo brakes. The 43-mm Showa GD 081 fork provided 130 mm of travel, while the fully adjustable rear Showa GD 082 gave 148 mm of wheel travel through its 65-mm stroke. Rigidity was further improved through 25-mm diameter axles front and rear. The Sport Touring wheels were three-spoke Brembo, a 3.50x17-inch and 5.50x17-inch, but with the release of the ST4 for the 1999 model year, they were now constructed of a new alloy with less silicon (GA/Si7). The new wheel rims were lighter, by 14 ounces (400 grams) in the

front and 31.5 ounces (900 grams) in the rear. Though appearing insignificant, this reduction in rim weight improved the steering and handling by reducing the gyroscopic effect as well as unsprung weight. The braking system consisted of the usual stainless steel, twin 320-mm discs at the front, but with an 851/888-sized 245-mm disc at the rear. The front brake calipers were gold, four-piston Brembo P4.30–34, but with the wider caliper mounts standardized during 1999. With Ferodo Ferit I/D 450 FF brake pads, a Brembo PS 16-mm master cylinder, and rubber brake lines, the braking system was still lacking in power and feel. Although the fluid reservoirs were remotely located, there were still no adjustable levers on the ST4. Along with the larger rear disc came a Brembo 34-mm twin piston brake caliper up from 32-mm on the ST2 and a PS 11-mm master cylinder. The tire sizes were also shared with the ST 2 rather than the

916/996, a 120/70ZR17 on the front and a 170/60ZR17 on the rear. Like the other road bikes for the 1999 model year, the ST4 featured a new sidestand. A new gearshift lever came from the Monster and was a simple answer to earlier complaints that it was almost impossible to change gears with large touring boots. The design of the headlight now included vented piping to overcome fogging of the headlight lens. New colors—black and dark metallic blue or red or gray—set the ST4 apart visually from the ST2. However, apart from small decals on the tailpiece it was still very difficult to tell the two models apart.

Galluzzi paid considerable attention to ergonomics and practicality when designing the ST series. Even with a sporting chassis as a basis, he managed to integrate a semisporting riding position, provision for a passenger, and provision for full luggage into the design. The predecessor of the Sport

The ST4 instrument panel provided an up-to-date combination of analog and digital display. *Ian Falloon*

Touring was the 907 IE, descended from the Paso, with its full-covering bodywork over a rectangular section steel frame. The ST moved away from this and incorporated a full fairing that displayed both the engine and tubular steel frame. Although the fairing and headlight design wasn't as distinctive as the 916, aerodynamic testing provided more effective high-speed wind protection along with improved air flow. For the first time on a motorcycle, there were aspheric rear vision mirrors giving a wider field of vision. Another first for Ducati was the option of factory-fitted, color coordinated luggage. These Nonfango-

manufactured bags required the mufflers be positioned lower, but this was easily achieved as the muffler bracket was variable. One of the most intriguing features for a Ducati was a 916-derived instrument panel that not only incorporated an analog display but also a digital readout for information. This included fuel consumption and reserve, water temperature, and a clock.

There was no doubt that the ST4 filled an important niche in the Desmoquattro line-up. Although not traditionally the strongest sellers in the range, sport-touring motorcycles have always broadened the appeal of Ducati as a predominantly sporting marque. The new generation of sport-tourers has attracted first-time Ducati purchasers, and the ST2 and ST4 have provided Ducati with a more mainstream image. Part of this is due to their overall excellence in filling the roles for which they were intended, with the ST4 in particular offering an exceptional balance of comfort and performance. At 452 pounds (215 kilograms), the weight was moderate for the sport-touring category, and the ST4 also provided race-bred handling as expected f rom Ducati.

In response to criticism that the ST4 looked too similar to the ST2, there were revised decals for the 2000 model year. With its large "ST4" decals on the side of the

For the 2000 model year, larger decals distinguished the ST4 from its more mundane sibling, the ST2. The color coordinated saddlebags were an essential component for comfortable touring. *Ian Falloon*

fairing, it was now easily distinguished but there were also a number of functional improvements this year. From the 996 came thicker crankshaft shims, larger bearing shells, and new timing gears to match the larger main bearing bushing rings. There was a metal cylinder head gasket, a new cylinder assembly, and a modified flywheel to accommodate a new bushing on the starter clutch gear. The engine cases had a closed by-pass hole and there was a new oil pressure switch with modified calibration. Although the engine specifications were the same as before, the power was reduced to 105 horsepower at 9,000 rpm.

To further differentiate the ST2 and ST4, there were a number of chassis improvements specific to the Desmoquattro version. The front brakes now included 320-mm stainless steel discs with aluminum carriers, but on the ST4 these were 5 mm thick, rather than 4 mm, as on the ST2. The ST4 also featured braided steel front and rear brake lines and sintered Toshiba TT 2802 front brake pads, but there were still nonadjustable brake and clutch levers. These developments, however, definitely provided superior braking performance over the 1999 version. While the ST2 retained a PS 13-mm clutch master cylinder, the ST4 now used a smaller PS 12-mm to reduced lever effort. There was also a braided steel clutch line. Also for 2000 the rear tire was increased in size on the ST4, to 180/55 ZR17. Further distinguishing the two models was the Ducati Corse-inspired gunmetal gray frame and wheels on the ST4, while the ST2 retained the earlier bronze frame and wheels. Yellow replaced black and became one of the primary colors for the ST4.

All 2000 models received the new sidestand sensor and relay preventing the sidestand from automatically retracting. The sidestand now incorporated an ignition cut out and effectively satisfied the critics who had complained for this feature for many years. All STs featured a power outlet for electrical accessories such as electric vests, cellular phones, intercoms, and lights. The socket could also be used to connect a reverse flow battery charger to charge the battery. There was also a Kryptonite antitheft padlock housed in a recess under the seat, new wiring, and a "SPORTTOURING" logo in the fuel tank guard. The rear splash guard disappeared, but a practical feature in response to stones chipping the fairing was a double-layer protective transparent plastic coating.

With the release of the higher performance ST4S for the 2001 model year, the ST4 remained virtually unchanged. As the ST2 also received the gunmetal gray frame and wheels this year, the ST4 resumed its former status as that of an ST2 with a Desmoquattro engine. Engine developments for 2001 included larger, 12-mm engine mounts. This may have appeared an insignificant improvement, but in the case of the Sport Touring series, where the engine and swingarm were supported by only two frame mounts, this provided greatly increased torsion stiffness. There were also new oil pipe lines to the oil cooler with double O-rings for improved sealing at high pressures. The ST4 chassis specifications were slightly downgraded with an adjustable Sachs shock absorber and thinner, 4-mm front brake discs, but the ST4 remained a strong seller. A total of 4,896 were produced through the end of 2000. There were only minimal developments for 2002. Instead of a steel clutch housing and steel plates, these were now aluminum, and for non-U.S. versions there was a silencer with a Euro 2, standard compliant catalytic converter.

The ST4S

If ever there was a model that was eagerly awaited, it was the ST4S. As with the

Offering true Superbike performance in a sport-touring package, the ST4S of 2001 was possibly the most practical and effective of all Desmoquattros.
Franco Bartoli

ST4, there was inevitability about the ST4S' appearance. It wasn't a question of whether it would happen, only when. Since the release of the ST4, the Sport Touring market had become more competitive, and new machines like the Aprilia Futura and Triumph Sprint were redefining the performance parameters for this category. Thus it was no surprise to see the release of the ST 4S at the Munich Intermot toward the end of 2000.

Central to the ST4S was the 996-cc (98x66-mm) Desmoquattro power unit, essentially that of the sporting 996, but retuned to provide power midway between the 996 and the 996 S. To maintain the same weight distribution as the ST4, the ST4S also featured cylinder heads with a lowered exhaust camshaft. The camshaft timing was identical to the 996, with the same intake valve lift of 9.60 mm, and exhaust valve lift of 8.74 mm. The valve sizes were still 36 and 30 mm, and the compression ratio slightly higher at 11.2:1. The higher power output of 117 horsepower at 8,750 rpm came mainly through the revised fourth-generation Weber Marelli 5.9

M electronic injection system that, like the 996, fired twin simultaneous injectors. The 5.9 M CPU also incorporated an immobilizer function, and there was a new fuel pump with a lighter, more compact flange.

Although the gunmetal gray frame with new 12-mm engine bolts was the same as that of the ST4, the ST4S featured an aluminum swingarm. Other upgraded components included a 43-mm Showa fork with TiN coated stanchions, and an Öhlins rear shock absorber with a hydraulically operated remote spring preload adjuster. This was conveniently positioned on the right side, so that adjustment could be made even while on the move. Completing the chassis improvement were five-spoke Marchesini wheels, manufactured by Brembo. These saved 2.2 pounds (1 kilogram) in unsprung weight. Further setting the ST4S apart were thicker (5-mm) front brake discs, optional carbon-fiber fenders, and a high-quality Asahi-Denso switchgear. The color for the ST4S was either red, yellow, or titanium gray, with new graphics. With a dry weight of 469 pounds (212 kilograms), the ST4S was clearly the class leader of sport-tourers. Because production could barely keep up with demand, there were no changes apart from an aluminum clutch drum and plates for the 2002 model year.

The Monster S4

With the continued success of Miguel Galluzzi's Monster, it was no surprise to see this expand to include a Desmoquattro-powered version for the 2001 model year. However, the Desmoquattro Monster S4 was not a variant of the existing two-valve versions, but almost an all-new design. In many ways, the Monster S4 was an adaptation of the ST4, sharing its basic engine and frame architecture with the sport-touring model.

From the ST4 came the 916-cc Desmoquattro engine with lowered exhaust camshafts. As with the ST4, the more compact cylinder heads enabled the engine to be positioned farther forward for optimum weight distribution. Although the camshafts were the same, the engine was retuned to emphasize a broader powerband.

There were 40-mm exhaust header pipes, a larger airbox with a resonator, and a new Weber Marelli 5.9 M electronic engine management system, with a 50-mm throttle body. The single injector was positioned inside the throttle body and the 5.9 M system incorporated CAN logic and an immobilizer. All the electronic components were lighter and more compact than before, and the processor was a Motorola ALTAIR with 32-bit data processing and a 20-MHz clock. The new injection and ignition computer had four drivers piloting the injectors and another four managing the ignition coils. Many more variables could be incorporated. Signals were accepted by two lambda probes, with inputs for engine revs (up to 18,000 rpm), vehicle speed, water temperature, throttle position, air temperature and pressure, and the usual safety features such as stand and gearbox position. The ignition coils were cigar-type, inserted directly in the spark plug leads, into the heads. The capability of the 5.9 M was such that it still wasn't exploited to the fullest but could be adapted for future requirements.

It was inevitable that the Desmoquattro engine would make its way to the highly successful Monster family. This occurred for the 2001 model year, but there was more to the S4 than the simple installation of 916 engine in the Monster running gear. This is the Foggy Monster, but the frame and engine were essentially identical to that of the standard S4. *Ian Falloon*

The aesthetics on the left side of the engine were less satisfactory, as it was difficult to conceal the water pump and plumbing for the cooling system. *Ian Falloon*

The only engine specification that differed from the ST4 was the inlet camshaft, which closed the inlet valve earlier—61 degrees after bottom dead center. The gearbox ratios were also the same as the ST4 and the 2000 Model 996. There were carbon-fiber heat shields for the stainless steel exhaust pipes, and Monster 900 IE mufflers. With an 11:1 compression ratio, the power of the Monster S4 was lower than that of other 916s, but with 101 horsepower at 8,750 rpm it was still 23 horsepower up on the two-valve 900 IE.

One of the challenges facing the design team was the aesthetic adaptation of the liquid-cooled Desmoquattro engine to a naked motorcycle with the engine on full view. With Pierre Terblanche engaged on other projects, this was entrusted to the engineering department. On the right side, the battery was moved from its exposed position on the side of the engine to a mount behind the airbox, above the rear cylinder. The battery was also a much lighter, no-maintenance lead-gel type. With the engine finished in aluminum-gray, the right side aesthetics were improved with carbon-fiber timing belt covers. The left side with its exposed water pump presented even more of a challenge, but was enhanced with a new pump housing and engine cover, along with revised water pump hoses. Unlike other 916s, the Monster S4 had no external chin-mounted oil cooler, and this required an increase in the cooling system pressure to 17.4 psi (1.2 bar), from 13 psi (0.9 bar), with a corresponding increase in the water pump flow rate to 3.5 liters per minute (from 2.6) at 6,000 rpm. The thermostat also opened at 65 degrees Celsius instead of 75 degrees. While the Desmoquattro engine still hardly looked beautiful from the left side, it was an improvement.

Although the Monster S4 styling followed that of the two-valve Monsters, the frame was based on that of the ST4, with thicker (28x2-mm) tubing. Rather than the 23-degree steering head angle of other Monsters, the S4 had the same 24-degree angle as the ST4, and the engine was positioned 20 mm higher than the 900 IE Monster to improve ground clearance. The wheelbase was also lengthened .39 inches (10 mm), to 56 inches (1,440 mm), through a specially designed aluminum swingarm, to obtain evenly split weight distribution. Three-dimensional modeling was used to obtain the optimum design for sports riding with more than 100 horsepower, resulting in a swingarm that consisted of three sections. Two extruded rectangular section tubes were welded to a chill-cast central section.

The 43-mm Showa front fork was similar to those on the ST4, as were the Brembo brakes, apart from thicker disc rotors. These were 320x5 mm, with P4 30–34 calipers, a PSC 16-mm master cylinder, and braided steel brake lines. At the rear was an adjustable Sachs shock absorber with piggyback reservoir and the usual Monster brake setup of a 245-mm disc with a twin

piston caliper. For 2001, this was positioned on top rather than underneath the swingarm to reduce noise. The wheel travel was the same as other Monsters, 120 mm on the front and 144 mm on the rear, providing a slightly tighter feeling than the ST4. Separating the S4 from other Monsters were the five-spoke Marchesini wheels. There was also a choice of tire sizes, with either a 120/70x17-inch or 120/65x17-inch on the

Aldo Drudi-designed bodywork set the Foggy Monster apart from the standard S4. *Ian Falloon*

front, or a 180/55x17-inch or 190/50x17-inch on the rear.

For the 2000 model year, Pierre Terblanche gave the Monster range its first design update since its inception in 1992. Thus the Monster S4 followed this pattern, reflected particularly in the redesigned fuel tank, tail section, and front fender. Advanced Unigraphics software was used to generate computerized 3D modeling, resulting in considerably shorter development time. New for the S4 was the dashboard that incorporated a temperature warning light, two-piece handlebars that mounted directly on the top triple clamps, and racing-inspired PSC 12-mm clutch master cylinder. There was also carbon-fiber, on the fenders and side panels. With a dry weight of only 4.4 pounds (2 kilograms) more than the Monster 900 S, the 427-pound (193-kilogram) Monster S4 promised exciting and lively performance.

The S4 Fogarty

One of the most successful marketing moves by Ducati was the pioneering of the exclusive sale of limited-production

motorcycles via the Internet. The first of these was the Mike Hailwood *evoluzione,* which sold out within hours from its release on January 1, 2000. Later in that year the same principle was successfully applied to the new 996 R, followed in June 2001 by the Monster S4 Fogarty. The career of Carl Fogarty, the most successful racer ever for Ducati, came to a premature end in a freak accident early in the 2000 racing season. Since then, he has become an official ambassador for the marque. Italy honors its heroes and former champions, and "King Carl" is no exception. Thus was born the "Foggy" S4, a limited-edition Monster S4 celebrating Carl Fogarty.

Although the S4 Fogarty was ostensibly similar to the standard Monster S4, there were a number of developments to justify the hefty price of 18,000 Euros. The impetus for this project came from Daniele Casolari of Ducati Performance in October 2000. "From the outset, the Foggy Monster was a Ducati Performance venture, and I asked my friend, the renowned stylist Aldo Drudi, to create new color-coded bodywork,"

Casolari told the author. Drudi is a leader in style and well-known in Italy for his individual helmet and leather designs for top GP riders Mick Doohan, Valentino Rossi, and Max Biaggi. He reshaped the fuel tank, allowing the rider's knees to tuck in closer together, and gave the dual color seat a special nonskid fabric. Drudi then created a tricolor color scheme that coordinated the fuel tank, front fender, headlight fairing, seat cowl and footpeg brackets with the specially painted frame and wheels. There were also Foggy logos on the fuel tank and headlight fairing, plus a Ducati Corse decal on the front fender. Setting the machine off was a laser-etched titanium plaque designed by Poggipolini. Each plaque carried a Fogarty signature and serial number.

Additional carbon-fiber parts included twin radiator cowls, aimed at improving the aesthetics of the exposed radiator, a pair of air scoops to improve rear cylinder cooling, and a chin fairing bolted underneath the crankcase. Aerodynamically designed to enhance stability at high speed, this harked back to the days of the early 1980s, with the bevel-drive 900 and Mille S2. These also featured bellypans, but the Foggy S4 example was somewhat more subtle in its execution.

Unlike the standard Monster S4, the Foggy version received upgraded Showa 43-mm forks with plasma-sprayed TiN-coated fork legs to reduce stiction. Strangely, the rear shock absorber was the same Sachs unit as the base model, though the Foggy model received a carbon steering damper kit with a light alloy mount. The result was a reduction in weight to 418 pounds (189 kilograms), improving on-the-road performance. This was further enhanced through more horsepower. Although the internals of the 916-cc Desmoquattro engine remained unchanged, the optional high-level exhaust system with oval carbon-fiber Termignoni mufflers, Superbike-derived airbox design, and recalibrated CPU saw the power climb to 110 horsepower at 9,750 rpm. Combined with a lower final drive gearing through a 39-tooth ergal rear sprocket in place of the 37-tooth steel item, the Foggy Monster provided impressive acceleration. Completing the specification were front and rear paddock stands, and a special bike cover, complete with Foggy's staring eyes logo.

A special Termignoni exhaust system contributed to the improved performance of the Foggy Monster. *Ian Falloon*

Even though it didn't appear to offer that much more than a regular production Monster S4, and was one of the more expensive motorcycles offered, 142 of the 300 Fogarty S4s offered were sold within the first 24 hours of their release over the Internet on June 20, 2001. The first example went to a Japanese buyer.

Chapter Nine

Testastretta

Despite the continued success of the 996 on the racetrack and in the showroom, it was obvious this venerable design couldn't last forever. Even before Honda won the 2000 World Superbike Championship, Ducati was aware that time was running out for its Desmoquattro. Although the design that first appeared in 1986 as a 748 was still responding to continual development, the competition had finally caught up, and it was time for a re-evaluation of the concept.

Soon after Texas Pacific Group bought the company toward the end of 1996, the debate over the 916 replacement began in earnest. Initially there were calls for a completely new engine, and in early 1998 Ing. Massimo Bordi indicated to the author, "It will have horizontally split crankcases with plain main bearings, and the cylinders will be rotated around the crankcase to reduce the overall length, in the style of the Honda VTR1000." At that stage Bordi even mentioned the possibility of a narrower angle V-twin (75 degrees), gear drive overhead camshafts, and either electromagnetic or Formula One-style pneumatic valve actuation. This would have represented a huge departure for Ducati, a company long associated with both desmodromics and the 90-degree "L-twin," as the great engineer Fabio Taglioni coined it.

Ultimately the more radical ideas were discarded, with the sanctioning of a further evolution of the current Desmoquattro. As Massimo Bordi said, "Although we briefly considered reducing the cylinder angle, apart from the technical disadvantages such as the need for balance shafts to eliminate vibration, we decided that it would be a mistake in terms of philosophy. It was the same with a nondesmo engine. Ducati and desmo are synonymous. That's why we opted for evolution, not revolution."

Once the formula and design parameters for the new engine were established in early 1998, an outside consultant was engaged to design the desmodromic cylinder head. The use of outside consultants wasn't new to Ducati. Ricardo in England had produced the 350-cc Grand Prix three-cylinder engine in 1971, and the Bolognese engineer Renato Armaroli was responsible for the four-valve, belt-drive 500-cc V-twin Grand Prix engine of 1973. Even though Armaroli gained his experience working at Tecno with Formula 2 BMW engines, these designs proved disappointing. This was probably why Ducati didn't consider consultant subcontractors for another 25 years.

When it came to selecting a consultant, Ducati turned to retired Formula One Ferrari engineer Ing. Angiolino Marchetti. Marchetti came with over 30 years of experience with Ferrari and was associated with Ducati and

The Testastretta of 2001 represented the first redesign of the Desmoquattro since its inception in 1986. The more compact cylinder heads are clearly evident on this factory Superbike racing engine. *Ian Falloon*

Piero Ferrari's HPE (High Performance Engineering); additionally, he had experience with desmodromic valve gear. Back in the late 1980s Marchetti had been involved with Ferrari's desmodromic V-12 Formula One engine, which had 96 opening and closing rockers. The Ferrari desmodromic engine never raced. In the design of the Testastretta, Marchetti worked closely with Ing. Massimo Bordi, but died during 1999 without seeing the project to fruition.

It wasn't only the cylinder head that needed updating on the new engine. Although the 98x66-mm engine was revving safely to 12,500 rpm in racing guise, by the 2000 season Aprilia already had its short stroke RSV Mille SP (100x63.4 mm) homologated for World Superbike, and Honda had its VTR 1000 SP (100x63.6 mm). Ducati's search for higher revs, along with improved cylinder filling and combustion, led it to use a shorter stroke of 63.5 mm, almost identical to the older 888, allowing revs to climb beyond 13,000 rpm. With a 100-mm bore, the new engine displaced 998 cc.

One of the most important requirements in the design of the cylinder head was a

reduction in the earlier included valve angle of 40 degrees. This came from the Cosworth DFV of 30 years earlier and was hindering combustion with high compression ratios. It wasn't so difficult to design a new cylinder head with a narrower valve angle, but retaining desmodromic valve actuation with steep downdraft ports presented a challenge. Also, because the Desmoquattro was initially designed as a 748, the basic cylinder head architecture was still modeled around an engine with an 88-mm bore, further compromising its ultimate potential as a 996.

Marchetti and Bordi decided on a flatter, 25-degree included valve angle that, with the 2-mm larger bore, permitted oversized valves while still providing a high compression ratio with a flat-topped piston. The narrower valve angle required a complete redesign of the existing Desmoquattro rocker layout that located all four rockers inboard of the camshafts. With this design, the opening, finger-type rockers were positioned directly above the closing, forked rockers. On Bordi's original thesis example of 1975, all four rockers were located outboard of the camshafts, but this resulted in a flatter port

Apart from the cylinder heads, the Testastretta engine of the 996 R featured a deeper sump extension. *Ian Falloon*

angle than was typical of that period. Marchetti's solution was to combine Bordi's two systems, with the opening rocker arms relocated outward to the front and rear edges of the cambox, with the closing rockers kept inside. The difficulty came with the support of the closing arms inside the head while maintaining a central spark plug. Marchetti's solution was to insert a central cast-steel sleeve for the spark plug, also using a single 10-mm spark plug instead of the previous 12-mm. On the top of each spark plug cap were F1-type stick coils.

As this new engine would eventually power a new range of motorcycles, it was important that the overall cylinder head be more compact. Thus the engine was titled *Testastretta,* which means narrower—and also slimmer as in diet—head. Thinning the internal water jackets reduced the overall dimensions, and all the internal components were lighter than before. The opening rocker arms were 50 percent lighter, and the closing rockers 20 percent lighter, without compromising strength. An important development was the arrangement of the rocker arm axes to provide symmetrical opening, always a problem on the earlier Desmoquattro. The new arrangement optimized the side thrust on the valves. Thanks to improved tooling, the rocker arm pad now matched the cam continuously throughout its rotation, resulting in considerably reduced clearance between the valve adjusters and rocker arms. The valve guides and seats were then machined simultaneously for perfect valve sealing.

Because considerable effort was spent on developing new desmodromic camshaft profiles, the camshafts also featured a larger outside diameter, and were hollow inside. The camshaft steel was no longer case hardened, but hardened and tempered, then nitrided after machining. These stronger camshafts were then bolted down, rotating directly in plain bearings in the cylinder head. This not only saved the weight and unnecessary inertia of the multiple roller bearings, but also made for a much more compact setup and reduced noise. Contributing further to the compactness of the cylinder head design, and simplifying maintenance, were single removable automotive-type valve covers.

The larger bore and shallower valve angle allowed for larger valves than on the 996. The 40-mm intake valves were inclined at 12 degrees, and the 33-mm exhaust valves were inclined at 13 degrees. Wave, a complex calculation system combining camshaft lobe design software with fluid-dynamic ducting process analysis, allowed the camshaft lobes to be more accurately matched in pairs. There was also new camshaft timing and valve lift, with the inlet valve opening 16 degrees before top dead center and closing 60 degrees after bottom dead center. The exhaust valve opened 60 degrees before bottom dead center, closing 18 degrees after top dead center. Because of the new camshaft lobe design, these figures were now taken at zero clearance. The valves also opened more than on the 996 SPS, the inlet opening 11.7 mm and the exhaust 10.1 mm.

Another advantage of the 996 R Testastretta cylinder head design was steeper, more downdraft porting to give the mixture a straighter path to the valves. The intake port angle was now 42 degrees from the horizontal, compared to the 35 degrees on the 996 SPS, while the exhaust port angle was 27.5 degrees as opposed to the earlier horizontal ports. The 996 R intake ports also were larger, increasing from 29 to 33 mm, while the exhaust port was reduced to 27.5 mm (from 29 mm). The intake manifolds were now manufactured from a highly corrosion-resistant polymer, Viton. A labyrinth seal molded in the manifold eliminated other seals between the flange and cylinder head.

While the Testastretta retained toothed belt drive to the four overhead camshafts, this also was improved. One of the design weaknesses of the earlier Desmoquattro was always the extreme angle between the upper timing belt pulleys. The new system used lower positioned pulleys with a revised belt tensioning system. The keyed pulleys on the camshafts were divided in two, enabling the belt to turn without pulling the camshaft during tensioning adjustment. An advantage of the new belt drive was a plus or minus two-degree accuracy of the camshaft lobe positioning in relation to top dead center of the piston. Thus, the safe minimum clearance between the piston and valves could be increased slightly, particularly on racing engines with extremely high compression ratios.

Earlier experience with the Supermono, with 100- and 102-mm pistons, taught Bordi much about attaining high revs with large pistons, and the 996 R featured 100-mm Asso pistons. These incorporated a single long relief in the flat top on either side for the valves, rather than the four individual pockets on the 996 SPS pistons. Providing a compression ratio of 11.4:1, the new 100-mm pistons were also one ounce (30 grams) lighter than their 98-mm predecessors. They still employed three Japanese-made rings, but to reduce blow-by oil loss, the oil ring comprised three separate segments rather than a single spring-loaded type. The con-rods were still Pankl titanium, and the new Nikasil-coated cylinders (still a closed deck-type) with their narrower water passages were much more compact. Apart from a shorter stroke, the crankshaft also had a spline, nut, and lock washer coupling for the primary drive, rather than the taper and key system. This was similar to the racing 996.

For the first time since the modified Pantah six-speed large crankcase design appeared in 1988, there were redesigned crankcases. These were sand-cast on the first examples, and still vertically split as the near-horizontal front cylinder prevented easy implementation of a horizontally

Even more exotic than the 996 R was the 998 R for 2002. This was powered by a short-stroke 999-cc Testastretta engine and featured more carbon-fiber bodywork. *Ian Falloon*

split crankcase. The cylinders were rotated 10 degrees backward to assist gravity oil scavenging from the front cylinder. More significant though was the integration of a *coppa bossa*, or bottom cup, as an integral component in the design of the externally reinforced crankcases. This had been a feature of racing engines since 1998. As the oil pump pickup was much lower, oil suction and consequent flow was now continuous even under the extreme conditions of heavy acceleration, wheelies, cornering, and late braking. The earlier Desmoquattro engine was prone to sucking air under high G-forces, resulting in oil starvation and engine failure.

As the camshafts now rotated in plain bearings, a more efficient oil filter was required, along with a revision of the lubrication system and an increase in oil pressure. In addition to the regular spin-on type of oil filter, there was now a vertically mounted cylindrical gauze filter in the base of the sump of the left crankcase half. On the previous Desmoquattro (996), oil to the camshafts and rocker arms was taken before reaching the oil cooler, while on the Testastretta (998) the oil feed to the cylinder head came from the circuit feeding the cooler to the crankshaft. This enabled cooler, and thus more viscous, oil to be supplied to camshaft bearings and rockers.

The six-speed gearbox was largely unchanged. The crankcases were still not designed to accept a side-loading gearbox, and to alter the internal ratios for racing still meant splitting the engine cases. However, the transmission output shaft was now supported by a double-row ball bearing with the countershaft sprocket fastened by a nut rather than a splined plate. There was also a refined, electrical contact, neutral indicator sensor on the gear selector drum. The dry multiplate clutch was similar to that of the 996 SPS, and still without the slipper arrangement featured on the 748 R. The result of these developments saw the Testastretta engine weighing in at 157 pounds (71 kilograms), 6.6 pounds (3 kilograms) less than the engine of the 996 SPS.

Also new was the 5.9 M Marelli electronic ignition and injection control unit. This more compact Marelli C 29 M unit was 2.8 ounces (80 grams) lighter than the P8 CPU, with a 20-Mhz processor, rather than the earlier 16-Mhz. The memory was increased

Even lighter Marchesini wheels and more offset front discs for improved cooling were new for the 998 R. *Ian Falloon*

from 8 to 32 MB and the system provided more efficient engine management. Rather than the P8 system, which used a separate rpm sensor and injection timing sensor, the 5.9 M was similar in design to the 1.6 M with a single inductive pickup. This faced the timing gear, reading the 46 teeth and a gap equal in size to two teeth, but still required accurate meshing of the crankshaft and timing gears to provide perfect rpm information.

The throttle bodies were increased to 54 mm, with elliptical chokes, rather than the 50-mm cylindrical chokes of the 996 SPS. Like the factory 996 racers and the 748 R, the 996 R utilized a single, centrally positioned, external F1-style raindrop spray-type injector per cylinder. These injectors were mounted in plastic retainers over the throttle bodies. With oval aluminum mufflers, the resulting Testastretta engine as fitted to the production 996 R provided 135 horsepower at 10,200 rpm. This was 10 percent more than the 996 SPS. Each 996 R also came with an optional power kit that included Termignoni carbon-fiber mufflers and ECU remapping, providing an additional six horsepower.

The 996 R

Although the Testastretta was to be the engine spearheading Ducati's performance line-up for the future, full-scale production couldn't initially be implemented. In the interim, the Testastretta was placed in the current 996 chassis. This saw the creation of the 996 R, replacing the 996 SPS as the Desmoquattro range leader, and maintaining a tradition retaining the earlier model designation even though the displacement was increased. Apart from the new engine there were also a few developments to the chassis. The 996 R frame was a modified Fogarty-type, constructed of 2-mm-diameter chrome-molybdenum tubing, with an aluminum rear subframe and 12-mm engine mounting bolts. While the 43-mm Öhlins

fork, Öhlins shock absorber, and five-spoke Marchesini wheels were similar to those of the 996 SPS, the front brakes were upgraded on the 996 R. The quest to further reduce unsprung weight saw thinner (4.5-mm instead of 5-mm) 320-mm front discs with nine ergal floating fasteners connecting the lightweight ergal disc carrier to the steel rotor. Each disc weighed 23.8 ounces (680 grams), saving 14 ounces (400 grams) overall, with the pad contact area reduced from 36 mm to 34 mm. There also were new-generation "triple-bridge-type" four-pad Brembo front brake calipers with four 34-mm pistons. Also new was the front master cylinder, a PSC 15/25 with a 15-mm piston instead of the previous 16-mm. The new master cylinder was designed to provide the leverage of a smaller piston, but with less effort and a more linear feel. Although visually the 996 R looked similar to the 996 SPS, the new carbon-fiber fairing no longer incorporated side vents. The sleeker new shape reduced the drag coefficient by 0.02 Cx points. The dry weight of 409 pounds (185 kilograms) also made the 996 R the lightest large-displacement Desmoquattro ever.

As with the 996 R, the 998 R featured a carbon-fiber fairing, the carbon-fiber is easily visible beneath the logo cutouts. *Ian Falloon*

Built as a limited production of 500 units for 2001, 350 996 Rs were sold immediately over the Internet on its release on September 12, 2000. The other 150 were retained for racing homologation, but these didn't feature individually numbered plaques. Also, because of difficulties regarding street homologation, all U.S. examples came without lights and stands, though the wiring remained in place.

Following its success in the 2001 World Superbike Championship, the Testastretta engine formed the basis of the entire large displacement Superbike line-up for 2002. The series had a generic title of 998 but one of the more surprising developments was the release of a second generation Testastretta, the 999. This was fitted to the limited production 998 R and as with the 996 R, the model designation didn't reflect the actual capacity. The 998 R Testastretta featured an even larger bore and shorter stroke, with 104-mm pistons and a 58.8-mm stroke. With

an even higher compression ratio of 12.3:1, the power of the 999-cc engine was increased 3 horsepower over the 996 R to 139 horsepower at 10,000 rpm. Still retaining the low sump sand-cast crankcases and 54-mm throttle bodies with a single shower injector, this engine was slated to power the next generation 999 Desmoquattro from 2003.

In most other respects, the 998 R was similar to the earlier 996 R, sharing the chrome-molybdenum frame, and TiN-coated Öhlins fork and Öhlins shock absorber. The Marchesini wheels were even lighter than those on the 996 R (by 14 ounces or 400 grams on the front and 28 ounces or 800 grams on the rear), and the 4.5-mm brake discs were in a more offset position to provide improved cooling. The fairing was still carbon-fiber, but to further reduce weight there was also a carbon-fiber tailpiece, without air intakes. Thus, the 998 R was even lighter than its predecessor, at 404 pounds (183 kilograms).

One of the most desirable motorcycles in the world during 2001 was the 996 R. Only 500 were manufactured, with 350 sold over the Internet during September 2000. *Ian Falloon*

In a pattern replicating the 996 S of 2001, the 998-cc 996 R Testastretta engine now made its way to the 998 S, except on models destined for the United States.

However, unlike the slightly lower-specification version of the 2000 model year 996 SPS engine that powered the 2001 996 S, the 998 S engine was identical to that which powered the highly expensive limited production 996 R. This retained the sand-cast low-sump crankcases, Marelli 5.9 M electronic injection system with 54-mm throttle bodies and a single shower injector, and larger capacity airbox. With 136 horsepower at 10,000 rpm, the 998 S was 13 horsepower up on the 2001 model year 996 S. The U.S. specification 998 S received the 123-horsepower Testastretta engine, as

There may have been a Testastretta engine lurking underneath the bodywork, and the fairing lacked upper air scoops, but the 996 R still bore a strong resemblance to the original 916 of 1994. *Ian Falloon*

the 136-horsepower engine couldn't pass the strict EPA requirements.

When it came to the chassis, the 998 S, while not as highly specified as the 996 R, also represented an improvement over the 996 S. The 43-mm TiN-coated Showa forks and Öhlins shock absorber from the 2001 996R were retained, but the racing frame and improved front brakes came from the 996 R. The discs were 4.5 mm thick and the calipers were "triple-bridge" four-pad Brembo with four 34-mm pistons. The front master cylinder was a PSC 15/25 with a 15-mm piston. The 996 R-style fairing, constructed of a techno-polymer with a carbon-fiber belly pan, provided improved aerodynamics by eliminating the side vents. Available in red or yellow as either a Monoposto or Biposto, the 998 S weighed 413 pounds (187 kilograms).

The 998 replaced the base 996 for 2002. Although it used a Testastretta engine, it featured die-cast crankcases without the *coppa bossa* sump extension of the 998 R and 998 S. It shared the Marelli 5.9 M

For 2002, the 136-horsepower 996 R Testastretta engine made its way to the 998 S. The chassis specification, however, carried over from the earlier 996 S. *Ian Falloon*

The 998 replaced the 996 for 2002. This also had a Testastretta engine, but without the deep sump. *Ian Falloon*

injection system with 54-mm throttle bodies, single shower type injector, and larger capacity airbox with the other Testastrettas. With 45-mm exhaust pipes, the 998 produced 123 horsepower at 9,750 rpm. Most of the chassis components were carried over from the 996 of 2001 except for the 996 R-type frame, new fairing without side vents, and 4.5-mm front brake discs. The weight also remained at 438 pounds (198 kilograms). Revised graphics graced the entire 2002 model year Superbike line-up.

Ducati offered two more limited edition 998s for 2002. At Ducati Revs America in

Las Vegas on October 26, 2001, a 998 S Bostrom replica was unveiled. There were to be three series of 155 units (Bostrom's racing number) for the United States, Europe, and the rest of the world. Although the U.S. versions received the 123-horsepower engine, to compensate, they were fitted with a carbon-fiber fairing, belly pan, front shield, airbox, under-seat heat guard, and fender. The two other series had the 136-horsepower engine but less carbon-fiber. Racing-inspired graphics and Öhlins front forks, and an Öhlins steering damper set all Bostrom replicas apart from the standard 998 S.

At the Bologna Motorshow, soon after the announcement of the 998 S Bostrom, Ducati unveiled the 998 S Bayliss, created to celebrate Bayliss' victory in the 2001 World Superbike Championship. Unlike the 998S Bostrom, the Bayliss was offered for sale only over the Internet. The specifications were identical to the 998 S Bostrom, with the United States receiving the lower-horsepower engine and more carbon-fiber. Setting the Bayliss apart was a signature on each fuel tank. Projected production was 300, with provisions to boost production up to a maximum of 500 units.

Now into its ninth year of production, the 916/996/998 still manages to reign supreme and has established itself as one of the all-time great motorcycle designs. History may well judge the 916/996/998 as the pinnacle of late-1990s motorcycle engineering. However, despite its brilliance, the design couldn't remain supreme forever. As it approached a decade of production, the 998 was no longer the lightest and fastest Superbike, and by 2001 Ducati's design director, Pierre Terblanche, had already prepared a replacement Desmoquattro to spearhead the line-up through the next decade.

For 2003, the 999 promises to uphold and extend the tradition of the Desmoquattro that began its life back in 1986. The 999 will be lighter and smaller, embracing new electronic and suspension technology, with adjustable ergonomics that will cater to a wider range of riders. Terblanche showed that a small motorcycle such as the Supermono can be designed to comfortably cater to riders of all sizes, and so it will be with the 999.

A new era for the Desmoquattro is about to begin, and it will surely continue to be the world's premier sporting motorcycle.

Index

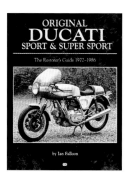

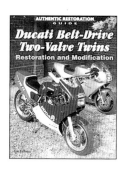

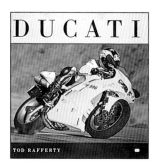